TRAVELLERS

VIETNAM

GW00418148

By
MARTIN HASTINGS

Written by Martin Hastings
Updated by David Henley

Photography by CPA Media

Editing and page layout by Cambridge Publishing Management Ltd,
Unit 2, Burr Elm Court, Caldecote CB23 7NU
Series Editor: Karen Beaulah

Published by Thomas Cook Publishing
A division of Thomas Cook Tour Operations Ltd
Company Registration No. 1450464 England

PO Box 227, The Thomas Cook Business Park,
Coningsby Road, Peterborough PE3 8SB, United Kingdom
E-mail: books@thomascook.com
www.thomascookpublishing.com
Tel: +44 (0)1733 416477

ISBN: 978-1-84157-800-2

Text © 2007 Thomas Cook Publishing
Maps © 2007 Thomas Cook Publishing
First edition © 2005 Thomas Cook Publishing
Second edition © 2007 Thomas Cook Publishing

Project Editor: Sasha Heseltine
Production/DTP Editor: Steven Collins

Printed and bound in Italy by: Printer Trento.

Front cover credits, L–R © John Banagan/Getty Images; © Morandi
Bruno/SIME-4Corners Images; © Damm Stefan/SIME-4Corners Images
Back cover credits, L–R © Gavin Hellier/Getty Images;
© John Banagan/Getty Images

Contents

KEY TO MAPS

✈   Airport

▲
Mt. Fansipan   Mountain

★   Start of walk/tour

Hwy-1
RN-9   Road numbers

Introduction

Vietnam has crept up relatively suddenly in the world's tourist consciousness. Until recently, the mainstream view was that Vietnam was one of those exotic, mysterious countries that always fascinated you but which you would never be likely to visit. Suddenly, it is seen as the next hip destination for travellers of all ages and budgets. Well, the truth is that Vietnam is a stunning package, a veritable delight of rich culture and vibrancy, just waiting to be opened.

The stereotypical images of Vietnam in Western popular consciousness are well known: verdant paddy fields studded with the conical hats of local farmers;

smiling schoolgirls breezing by on creaking bicycles wearing traditional *ao dai* tunics; colonial Europeans wearing white linen suits edging their way through crowded Asian alleyways; and of course the searing, tragic images from countless Hollywood movies of the 'Vietnam War'.

These images of Vietnam do not reflect the richness and diversity of the new Vietnam. As the number of tourists finding their way here soars, the word is out that this is a land not of bomb craters, but of sugar-white beaches, vibrant cities and venerable pagodas. The speed with which Vietnam's population of 77 million has been able to transcend the recent past comes as a surprise to visitors who are met with warmth and curiosity rather than resentment.

Vietnam is experiencing economic change at a pace that leaves you breathless – it has one of the fastest-growing economies in the world. This is a country that appears to be

Communist in name only, where everyone it seems is a shop-keeper or an entrepreneur.

Vietnam is, to use the cliché, 'a land of contrasts'. Its appeal lies in the mixture of traditional customs with economic growth, values and beliefs that are typically Asian mixed with a fascination with all things Western. Travellers who believe that Thailand has seen its best years come and go should be making tracks for Vietnam. The country is emerging from its draconian past to embrace capitalism and tourism with equal fervour. Vietnam is a young country where a large percentage of the population is under the age of 25. Long closed to the outside world, it retains a charming innocence that most tourist regions lack. Yet in the decade since the country opened its doors to visitors, the country has built world-class hotels and tourism facilities of international standards and traditional Vietnamese hospitality.

Vietnam's culture comes in a stunning package. The country extends for about 1,650km (1,025 miles) along the eastern coast of the Indochinese Peninsula. The people describe their country as a bamboo shoulder pole slung with two baskets of rice – the fertile southern Mekong Delta and the northern Red River Delta. From these lowland paddy fields stretch vast rubber plantations, rolling hills covered with thick jungle, and jagged mountains standing more than 3,000m (9,843ft) high. Over 3,200km (1,988 miles) of coastline features endless stretches of white sand beaches.

As well as fine weather, there is spectacular natural scenery and historic sites. Vietnam is a country with a past as rich as the soil in the blazing green deltas. Traditions carry real meaning. Ancient heroes are still venerated at colourful temple festivals, people honour their ancestors, and village elders teach values of hard work, hospitality and filial loyalty. With 54 ethnic groups, most of whom live in remote areas and follow age-old customs, Vietnam offers unparalleled opportunities for cultural exploration.

Introduction

Boats on the Perfume River, near Hué

The land

The Socialist Republic of Vietnam, a sovereign and reunified independent country, is located in the centre of Southeast Asia, and is shaped like the letter 'S'. The country lies in the eastern part of the Indochina peninsula, and is bordered by China to the north, and Laos and Cambodia to the west. The country's total length, from the northernmost point to the southernmost point, is 1,650km (1,025 miles).

Geography

Vietnam has a high percentage of territorial waters, with a coastline measuring 3,260km (2,026 miles). Its width, stretching from east to west, is 600km (373 miles) at the widest point in the north, 400km (249 miles) in the south, and 50km (31 miles) at the narrowest part on the central coast.

The country's two main cultivated areas are the Red River Delta (15,000sq km/5,400sq miles) in the north and the Mekong Delta (60,000sq km/23,400sq miles) in the south. Three-quarters of the country is mountainous and hilly; the highest peak, at 3,143m (10,310ft), is Fansipan in northwest Vietnam.

Vietnam's range of topography allows for an incredibly varied travel experience. The country is made up of equatorial lowlands, high, temperate plateaux and cooler mountainous areas.

Lying in the intertropical zone, local conditions vary from frosty winters in the far northern hills to the year-round warmth of the Mekong Delta.

Flora and fauna

Vietnam's wildlife is in decline due to the destruction of habitats, illegal hunting and pollution. Fauna includes elephants, rhinoceros, tiger, leopard, black bear, snub-nosed monkey, crocodile and turtle. Less than 30 per cent of the country remains forest-covered, and what remains is under threat from population pressure and the growth of industry. The situation has improved since 1992 following new education programmes and reforestation projects, and the banning of unprocessed timber exports.

Despite being little visited by travellers, Vietnam has ten national parks and an expanding array of nature reserves. The most interesting and accessible national parks are Cat Ba, Ba Be Lake and Cuc Phuong in the north, Bach Ma in the centre and Nam Cat Tien and Yok Don in the south. In an attempt to prevent an ecological and hydrological catastrophe, the government has plans to improve existing parks and open up new ones.

Vietnam

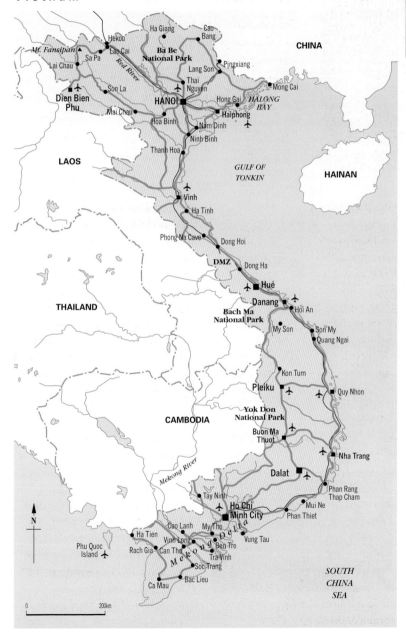

CHINA

Ha Giang
Cao Bang
Hekou
Mt. Fansipan
Sa Pa
Lao Cai
Ba Be National Park
Lai Chau
Red River
Lang Son
Pingxiang
Son La
Thai Nguyen
Mong Cai
Dien Bien Phu
HANOI
Hong Gai
HALONG BAY
Mai Chau
Haiphong
Hoa Binh
Nam Dinh
Ninh Binh
Thanh Hoa
GULF OF TONKIN
HAINAN

LAOS

Vinh
Ha Tinh
Phong Na Cave
Dong Hoi
DMZ
Dong Ha
Hué
THAILAND
Danang
Hoi An
Bach Ma National Park
My Son
Son My
Quang Ngai
Kon Tum
Pleiku
Quy Nhon
Yok Don National Park
CAMBODIA
Buon Ma Thuot
Nha Trang
Mekong River
Dalat
Tay Ninh
Phan Rang Thap Cham
Ho Chi Minh City
Mui Ne
Phan Thiet
Cao Lanh
My Tho
Vung Tau
Ha Tien
Vinh Long
Ben Tre
Rach Gia
Can Tho
Tra Vinh
Mekong Delta
Phu Quoc Island
Soc Trang
Bac Lieu
Ca Mau
SOUTH CHINA SEA

N

0   200km

The environment

Vietnam is endowed with a rich variety of wildlife as well as some stunning primeval forests. However, the ravages of war and deforestation have created a large number of issues for the environment. Slowly, the government is realising the economic value of conservation, ecotourism and biodiversity.

Biodiversity

In recent years, the scientific community has been excited about the identification of several species of mammal and bird previously unknown to the world. Vietnam has a wide variety of primates and bird species, with about 16,000 plant and 2,500 fish species. This biodiversity is largely due to the range of habitats that exists in the country, from the mountains in the north and the mangrove swamps in the Mekong Delta to the long eastern

All the national parks have a wide variety of flora and fauna

coastline. However, there are also many threatened species, including 40 types of mammals and 37 types of bird. Population growth, pollution, poaching and logging have all contributed to this conservation crisis.

In 1994, Vietnam signed an international convention outlawing trade in endangered species, and has established 87 nature reserves covering 3 per cent of the country's land. It is hoped that rare animals such as the Java rhinoceros and the kouprey (forest ox) will survive under this protection. In 2005 the government introduced a new Law on Tourism, which includes some hard-hitting regulations on pollution caused by tourism.

Ecocide

The 'American War' was tragic not only in terms of human cost and suffering, but also because of the impact of bombing on the environment. The word 'ecocide' was coined to describe the dropping of herbicides on forest and food crops to deprive the Viet Cong of forest cover.

The most notorious defoliant was Agent Orange, named after the colour of its storage containers. The dioxin within it is a powerful poison

A gibbon in the trees at Cuc Phuong

Since the war, extensive reforestation programmes have helped to regenerate the worst-affected areas. In 1987, 500 million trees were replanted. One of the major successes was the return of the Sarus crane to the Mekong Delta, which had abandoned its nesting grounds during the war.

that kills vegetation, staying active for up to ten years in the environment, and longer in human tissue. Over 40 million litres (8.8 million gallons) of Agent Orange were sprayed over the countryside in the 1960s, destroying half of Vietnam's mangrove swamps and a quarter of its forests. Crops were damaged, leaving people malnourished, while many villagers died from being sprayed or from drinking contaminated water. The dioxins also caused a high degree of miscarriage, birth defects and cancers, affecting up to 1 million Vietnamese.

Conventional bombing, totalling around 13 million tonnes of explosive, also wrought havoc on the land, to the extent that nothing will grow in some areas.

The effects of this devastation continue to be felt today. Large areas around the DMZ, in the centre of the country, the scene of the most savage fighting, are still bare of forests. The ground is still so polluted that only very hardy vegetation can grow.

Deforestation

The other environmental issue concerning Vietnam is deforestation, mainly due to commercial logging, firewood collection and agricultural clearance. Over the last 20 years, as much forest has been lost due to these causes as through the devastation caused during the American War. Only 30 per cent of the country's land is now covered by forest, down from 44 per cent in 1945. The worst-affected areas are in the northern mountains and the central highlands, where soil erosion and flooding are serious problems. In the highlands, tea, coffee and cocoa plantations are replacing the natural forests, in order to provide income for local communities, an issue that is causing conflict between the government and the ethnic minorities of the area. However, government conservation programmes are hoping to create sustainable forests, involving local communities, and increase the amount of forest to 40 per cent.

History

The most significant period in Vietnam's early history began in about 2000 BC with the emergence of a highly organised society of rice farmers, the Lac Viet, who are held to be the original Vietnamese nation.

In 111 BC, the Han emperors annexed the whole Red River Delta and so began a thousand years of Chinese domination. They introduced Confucianism and with it a rigid, feudalistic hierarchy dominated by a mandarin class.

The local aristocracy increasingly resented their Chinese rulers and engaged in various insurrections, culminating in the battle of the Bach Dang River in AD 938. A famous victory for Ngo Quyen, leader of the Vietnamese forces, led to his declaring himself ruler of Nam Viet, heralding what was to be nearly ten centuries of Vietnamese independence.

Meanwhile, in the south of Vietnam it was the Indianised kingdom of Champa that dominated the region until the late 10th century. The Champa people lost their territory north of Hué to the Viets, and four centuries later the whole kingdom became a Vietnamese state.

For the next ten centuries Dai Viet (Great Viet) was ruled by a series of dynasties. The most important were the Ly dynasty, who founded the city of Thang Long (the precursor of modern Hanoi), the Tran dynasty, who repelled three successive Mongol invasions, and the Later Le dynasty, who reconstructed the nation after a brief relapse into Chinese rule from 1407 to 1428. As the Later Le declined in the 16th century, two powerful clans took over, splitting the country in two. The Trinh lords held sway in Hanoi and the north, while the Nguyen set up court at Hué. The Nguyen lords conquered the Mekong Delta, and by the mid-18th century Viet people occupied the whole peninsula.

In 1771, three disgruntled brothers began the Tay Son rebellion, based on values of equal rights, justice and liberty. By 1788 they had overthrown both the Trinh and Nguyen lords. One of the few Nguyen lords to survive the Tay Son rebellion was Prince Nguyen Anh, who regained the throne in 1802 as Emperor Gia Long. For the first time Vietnam, as the country was now called, fell under a single authority. Gia Long established his capital at Hué, where he built a magnificent citadel in imitation of the Chinese emperor's Forbidden City. Gia Long and the Nguyen dynasty he founded reimposed the old feudal order, and gradually closed the country to the outside world.

In the 19th century, French governments began to see Vietnam as a potential route into the resource-rich provinces of southern China. By 1862 the French controlled the whole Mekong Delta and by 1887 the whole country, which they combined with Cambodia and, later Laos, to form the Union of Indochina. For the next 70 years Vietnam was once again under foreign occupation. The French launched a massive development of the country's infrastructure, funded by punitive taxes.

Until the mid-1920s Vietnam's various anti-colonial movements tended to be fragmented, but in 1925 the Revolutionary Youth League was founded over the border in southern China by Ho Chi Minh. In 1930 Ho persuaded the various rival anti-colonial movements to unite into one Indo-Chinese Communist Party, whose main goal was an independent Vietnam governed by workers, peasants and soldiers. In February 1941, Ho returned to Vietnam after 30 years in exile, joining other resistance leaders to forge a nationalist coalition, known as the Viet Minh. The organisation was specifically designed to win broad popular support for independence, followed by moderate social and democratic reforms. Over the next few years the Viet Minh established liberated zones in the northern mountains to provide bases for future guerrilla operations.

During the Second World War the country gradually fell under Japanese control. Upon the Japanese surrender in 1945 Ho Chi Minh called for a national uprising and on 2 September 1945 he proclaimed the establishment of the Democratic Republic of Vietnam. The Potsdam Agreement concluded at the end of the Second World War failed to recognise the new Republic. Instead,

History

The Hien Nhon Gate, which leads into the Forbidden Purple City, Hué

French troops remained, although France recognised the Democratic Republic as a 'free state' within the proposed French Union. However, it soon became apparent that the French were not going to abide by the treaty, and all-out conflict, known as the First Indochina War, broke out. The Viet Minh began to receive military aid from China and Russia from 1949; America was drawn into the war too, funding the French military effort. However, by 1953, France was tiring of the war. Losing the crucial battle of Dien Bien Phu was a nail in the coffin of French rule. Peace talks to end French occupation of Indochina began in Geneva just as the final French positions surrendered at Dien Bien Phu in early May, 1954.

The Geneva Conference succeeded only in reaching an interim solution, dividing Vietnam at the Seventeenth Parallel, pending nationwide free elections planned for July 1956 but never held. A demilitarised buffer zone was established to divide the Viet Minh in the North and the French in the South. The newly appointed prime minister of South Vietnam, anti-communist Ngo Dinh Diem, ousted Emperor Bao Dai and began silencing his many enemies, killing over 50,000 citizens in the process.

In Hanoi, meanwhile, Ho Chi Minh's government set about constructing a socialist society. Years of warring with France had profoundly damaged the country's infrastructure, and now it found itself deprived of the South's plentiful rice stocks. Conscription was introduced in April 1960, and the National Liberation Front (NLF) was created, which drew together all opposition forces in the South. Its guerrilla fighters were dubbed 'Viet Cong', or VC, Vietnamese Communists.

In early 1955, the White House began to bankroll Diem's government and the training of his army, the ARVN (Army of the Republic of Vietnam). Behind these policies lay the fear of the chain reaction that could follow in Southeast Asia, were Vietnam to be overrun by communism – the so-called 'Domino Effect'. Diem's brutally repressive government was losing ground to the NLF in the battle for the hearts and minds of the population. Buddhists were fired upon by ARVN soldiers in Hué, sparking off demonstrations against religious repression, and provoking a series of self-immolations by Buddhist monks. The US tacitly sanctioned a coup in 1963 that ousted Diem, who was captured and shot, but continued to back leaders in South Vietnam who were anti-communist, however corrupt or incompetent they were. American involvement in Vietnam gradually changed from economic and administrative support to full military involvement, leading to the most destructive and tragic period in Vietnam's history – the 'American War'.

At the end of the conflict the country was once again a unified nation, and in July 1976 the Socialist Republic of Vietnam was officially born. The economy in the South collapsed when the Americans left, based as it was on American funds and, in the words of journalist John Pilger, 'the services of maids, pimps, whores, beggars and black-marketeers'. The North meanwhile had no industry, a co-operative system of agriculture, and a land that had been bombed on a massive scale. A rigid socialist state was ushered in, with Hanoi the capital. Privately owned land was confiscated, collectivisation of agriculture was introduced, and as the state took control of industry and trade, output dwindled. Anyone with remote connections with America was interned in a 're-education camp', along with Buddhist monks, priests and intellectuals. Discrimination against those on the 'wrong side' in the war continues today.

The mess in which Vietnam found itself after reunification prompted many of its citizens to flee. From 1979 until the early 1990s alone, an estimated 840,000 of these 'boat people' arrived in 'ports of first asylum' such as Hong Kong. Pol Pot's genocidal regime in Cambodia was making cross-border forays into regions of Vietnam by 1976, leading to war. In 1978, Vietnamese troops invaded Cambodia and ousted Pol Pot. By the early 1980s the only thing keeping Vietnam afloat was Soviet aid. Finally, in 1986, Nguyen Van Linh introduced sweeping economic reforms, known as *doi moi* (renovation). Collectivisation and central planning were abandoned, a market economy was

embraced, agriculture and retail businesses were privatised, and attempts were made to attract foreign capital.

In 1993, the Americans lifted their embargo on aid, and Western investment began. Vietnam was admitted into ASEAN (the Association of Southeast Asian Nations) in 1995, and full diplomatic relations with the US were restored. By 1997 the economic honeymoon period was over. Economic growth flagged as foreign companies scaled back, frustrated by an overblown bureaucracy, and the economic crisis in Southeast Asia took hold.

National elections in 1997 ushered in the popular new prime minister, Phan Van Khai, who has continued both the economic reforms and the fight against corruption. One of the government's biggest problems is how to speed up the restructuring and privatisation of debt-ridden state enterprises. In the new millennium, there's no doubt a great deal has been achieved in Vietnam in a comparatively short time.

In 2000, President Clinton became the first US President to visit Vietnam in 25 years. Similar symbolic gestures, such as the visit of a US Navy ship to Ho Chi Minh city in 2003, are helping to bring the two nations together once again.

In a reciprocal gesture, Vietnamese Prime Minister Phan Van Khai made an important visit to the United States in 2005.

By 2006, Vietnam's staggering economic growth had brought it entry to the WTO (World Trade Organization).

The American War

The Vietnam conflict did not begin suddenly: it was a gradual process that first saw US military advisers and soldiers in Vietnam in the late 1950s, then escalated with the first US combat troops landing in Danang in 1965. The United States never officially declared war on North Vietnam.

The point of no return for the US came with the Gulf of Tonkin incidents in August 1964. American ships were allegedly attacked by the North Vietnamese Army (NVA), leading to Congress empowering

CHIẾN DỊCH ĐIỆN BIÊN PHỦ
VĨ ĐẠI ĐÃ TOÀN THẮNG

TIÊU DIỆT TRÊN 21 TIỂU ĐOÀN
VÀ 10 ĐẠI ĐỘI ĐỊCH GỒM
16 200 TÊN

A Communist Party war poster in the History Museum, Hanoi

President Johnson to deploy whatever means necessary 'to prevent further aggression' in Vietnam. Early 1965 saw the start of a sustained carpet-bombing campaign, which lasted three and a half years; twice the tonnage of bombs was dropped as had fallen in the whole of World War II. Despite this, the campaign failed to break the North's supply lines. NVA troops continued to infiltrate the South in increasing numbers, along the Ho Chi Minh Trail.

The number of American GIs in Vietnam increased each year, reaching half a million by 1967. Their mission was largely confined to keeping the NVA at bay in the central highlands and neutralising the guerrilla threat in the Viet Cong power-bases of the South. While the Americans had far superior resources, technology and fire power, the NVA were winning the crucial battle for the 'hearts and minds' of the local populations. Village people in South Vietnam found that they were better protected and treated by the NVA, who helped build tunnels, cultivate crops and keep food supplies hidden. In return, local villages fed and housed NVA patrols and supplied vital intelligence. Ordinary Vietnamese wanted to rid their country of foreign colonialists and return to their rural way of life.

The villages were also ideal recruiting stations for the NVA, who were seen by the local villagers as idealistic, disciplined, patriotic and simple country people just like them. Although the NVA cannot claim to have won many, if any, battles during the war, they had a virtually inexhaustible supply of troops. It is estimated that the North lost six troops for every one lost by the South.

The Tet Offensive in 1968 was a turning point in the war. In the early hours of 31 January a combined force of 70,000 NVA launched offensives on over a hundred towns across the South. The campaign failed to spark a hoped-for revolt against the American-backed regime and the VC was left with huge numbers of casualties. However, the effect of the war on US popular opinion was massive. Pictures and reports from the Tet Offensive shocked the US public so much that they demanded an end to the war. In March 1968, President Johnson announced a virtual cessation of bombing, and peace talks began a month later.

Under the terms of the Paris Accords, signed on 27 January 1973 by the United States, the North, the South and the Viet Cong, a ceasefire was established, and all remaining American troops were repatriated. Although the US pulled their troops

Vietnamese huddle in a trench during the American War

out, they continued to supply the South Vietnamese army (ARVN) and the war continued. While well armed and supplied, the ARVN did not have the same will or discipline to fight once the Americans began withdrawing their troops. They felt that they had always been fighting someone else's war. Towns in the South fell quickly, President Thieu fled the country, and Saigon fell to the Viet Cong on 30 April 1974.

The toll of the American War, in human terms, was staggering. Over 57,600 American troops died, and more than 150,000 received wounds which required hospitalisation. The ARVN lost 250,000 troops, while the communists lost one million. Over two million Vietnamese civilians died.

The astonishing postscript to the war is that few Vietnamese blamed the Americans for the conflict. To them, the war was 'the Will of Heaven', a tragic period of history that could not be attributed to any single cause.

History timeline

2000 BC   Emergence of the Lac Viet, a highly organised society of rice-farmers.

111 BC   The Han emperors from China annex the whole Red River Delta.

AD 938   Victory for Ngo Quyen at the battle of the Bach Dang River begins his rule over the Nam Viet, and nearly ten centuries of Vietnamese independence.

1788   Tay Son rebellion overthrows the Trinh and Nguyen lords.

1802   Emperor Gia Long regains the throne, establishing his capital at Hué, and founds the Nguyen dynasty.

1858   The French capture Da Nang, and subsequently gain control of the whole country, ruling for the next 70 years.

1925   Ho Chi Minh founds Vietnam's first Marxist-Leninist organisation, the Revolutionary Youth League.

1941   Ho Chi Minh returns to Vietnam after thirty years in exile, and forms the Viet Minh, a nationalist coalition against the French.

1945   Ho Chi Minh proclaims the establishment of the Democratic Republic of Vietnam.

1949   The communist victory in China leads to military support in the fight against the French.

1954   French defeat at the battle of Dien Bien Phu leads to French surrender and the Geneva Conference in which Vietnam is divided into two at the 17th parallel.

1956   Ngo Dinh Diem becomes Prime Minister of South Vietnam and begins his highly unpopular, repressive regime.

1960   National Liberation Front (NLF) is created in the North, dubbed the Viet Cong.

1964   US government allege unprovoked attacks on

their warships from North Vietnamese craft in the Gulf of Tonkin. President Johnson is given special powers 'to prevent further aggression'.

1965 The first US combat troops land in Danang, and the US start to bomb the Ho Chi Minh Trail, the North's supply route to the South.

1968 The Viet Cong launch the Tet Offensive, in which over a hundred towns across the South are attacked. Although militarily a failure for the Viet Cong, it succeeded in driving American public opinion against the war.

1973 The Paris Accords establish a ceasefire, although subsequent fighting sees the fall of Saigon to the North later in the year.

1976 The reunified Socialist Republic of Vietnam is officially born.

1979 The start of an exodus of Vietnamese 'boat people' to neighbouring countries.

1986 Nguyen Van Linh introduces sweeping economic reforms, known as *doi moi* or 'renovation'.

1995 Vietnam is admitted into ASEAN (the Association of Southeast Asian Nations) and full diplomatic relations with the US are restored.

1997 Phan Van Khai is elected as prime minister, promising to continue economic reforms and the fight against corruption.

2000 In a highly symbolic gesture, Bill Clinton becomes the first US President to visit Vietnam in over 25 years.

2006 Vietnam is admitted into the World Trade Organization (WTO).

War Remnants Museum, Ho Chi Minh City

Politics

The Socialist Republic of Vietnam (Cong Hoa Xa Hoi Chu Nghia Viet Nam) was born in July 1976, when the North and South of the country were unified after the American-backed South was defeated by the Communist North. The governance of Vietnam is characterised by a cumbersome, complicated system of politics and red tape. Officially the government is based on Marxist-Leninist philosophy, with the slogan 'Independence, Freedom, Happiness' (Doc Lap, Tu Do, Hanh Phuc), which you will see at the top of every official document.

Since the 1992 Constitution, there has been a separation of the Party and the State, which has caused a great deal of rivalry between the two. There are 25 official government ministries, all of which have a Party section. The army exerts a strong influence on the government, with most senior politicians coming from the national forces.

The state

The highest legislative authority of the state is the National Assembly, whose 500-odd deputies hold office for terms of five years. It is seen by many as just a rubber-stamp for initiatives coming out of the Communist Party. The National Assembly elects two bodies. The Council of State is like a collective presidency, whose 15 members carry out their duties when the National Assembly is not in session. The Council of Ministers acts like a Western-style cabinet.

Below the National Assembly there are local legislative bodies, the People's Councils that elect People's Committees, which hold a local executive role. In reality, there is rivalry between these two organisations at local level, which hampers decision-making.

The Party

The dominant political body is the Politburo. Its 19 members are nominated by the Central Committee of 125 members, who are in turn elected for five-year terms by the 1,000-member Congress. The influence of the Communist Party (Dang Cong San Viet Nam) can be felt at every level of the country's social and political life. The Party represents doctrine and knowledge, theoretically working in harmony with the State, representing administrative experience and power. In practice, there is conflict and rivalry at both local and national level.

The Party has a decentralised structure, which has given local leaders some leeway to develop local initiatives. However, corruption is a big problem, and crackdowns have been necessary in recent years to oust local Party officials who have ruled using extortion, terror and kidnapping. In addition, the 1980s and '90s saw the expulsion from the Communist Party of thousands of party members, to reduce corruption and make room for younger members.

In recent years Party Congresses, at which major policy changes are ratified, have been battlegrounds for disagreements between different factions. The main source of conflict has been over how quickly to modernise the country. The dogmatism and red tape that has put off many international investors in the past is slowly being dismantled to encourage more private enterprise and liberalise the economy in general.

Elections

Elections are held to select candidates for the National Assembly and local People's Committees. Everyone over 18 has to vote, although proxy voting is very common. The government is proud of its regular score of 100 per cent voter participation. Opposition parties are prohibited from running, with only Party-approved candidates allowed. Even independents need to have government approval to run.

The economy

Since 1997, Vietnam has made far-reaching structural reforms to facilitate the adoption of a market economy. Economic reforms and trade liberalisation have turbo-charged the economy to the extent that economic growth over the past few years has averaged an impressive 8 per cent. Joining the World Trade Organization in 2006 has opened up the country's markets to more American goods. So far it has done well to reduce population growth and rural poverty, but it is still a huge challenge to continue to privatise debt-ridden state enterprises without letting unemployment and economic inequality get out of control. With tourism and industry ever increasing, the gap between rich and poor is widening; the average monthly income for city dwellers is about US$100, but drops to US$30 in some rural provinces.

The Presidential Palace, Hanoi

Religion

The moral and religious life of most Vietnamese is governed by a mixture of four religions: Confucianism, Buddhism, Taoism and Christianity. Over the centuries, these have mixed with popular Chinese beliefs and ancient Vietnamese animism to form Tam Giao, *or the Triple Religion.*

Vietnam also has small Hindu, Muslim and Theravada Buddhist communities, as well as the second-largest Catholic population in Southeast Asia after the Philippines.

After 1975, the Communist government of reunified Vietnam declared the state atheist; churches and pagodas were closed down and religious leaders sent for re-education. Since 1986 the situation has eased, and many Vietnamese are once again openly practising their faith.

The role of religion

Most Vietnamese would say that they are Buddhists, but this is influenced by a variety of other beliefs, for example the Confucian system of social and political morality, and the Taoist conceptions of the cosmos. No matter what their religion, virtually every Vietnamese household maintains an ancestral altar for rituals associated with ancestor worship, which is based on the principles of filial piety and obligation to the past, present and future generations. Residual animism, plus spirits borrowed from other religions, further complicate Vietnam's mystical world, in which the universe is divided into three realms – sky, earth and man – under the guardianship of Ong Troi, Lord of Heaven.

Up to two-thirds of the Vietnamese population consider themselves Mahayana Buddhists, while at the same time adhering to a Confucian philosophy, whose emphasis on conformity and duty has played an essential role in Vietnam's political, social and educational systems. Many Taoist deities have been absorbed into other more mainstream cults, in particular Mahayana Buddhism.

Buddhism

The main form of Buddhism is Mahayana Buddhism, called Dai Thua or Bac Tong. The largest Mahayana sect is Zen, also known as the School of Meditation.

Buddhism was first introduced to Vietnam in the 4th century BC, and reached its peak in the Ly dynasty (11th century). It was then regarded as the official religion, dominating court affairs. Buddhism was preached broadly among the population and it exerted a profound influence on daily life. Many pagodas and temples were built during this time. At the end of the 14th century, Buddhism began to decline. The ideological influence of Buddhism, however, remains very strong in social and cultural life.

Confucianism

Brought to Vietnam by the Chinese in the 3rd century, Confucianism became the state philosophy in the 15th century. Confucian beliefs place an emphasis on human values such as duty, education and hard work, rather than a belief in heaven. The teachings of Confucius, a 6th-century BC Chinese humanist, are the foundation of Confucian beliefs, based on a social and political morality. Followers must respect the principles of goodness and justice and follow six moral virtues.

Christianity

Catholicism was introduced to Vietnam in the 17th century. During the presidency of Diem in the 1960s, Catholics received preferential treatment from the government, and some Vietnamese converted to Catholicism as a result. Before the 'American War', many Catholics in Northern Vietnam fled to the South to escape persecution from the Communists. About ten per cent of the population are Catholic.

Taoism

Created in China in the 6th century BC by Lao-tzu, a contemporary and adversary of Confucius, Taoism advocates the search for individual liberty in order to reach Tao, a morally correct path representing a harmonious universe, symbolised by masculine (the active yang) and feminine (the passive yin) forces. Among the many Taoist gods, those that tourists will most likely see include the Goddess of the Sea, Thien Hau Thanh Mau, and the Jade Emperor, Ngoc Hoang.

Other religious movements

Caodaism was first introduced to the country in 1926 by Ngo Van Chieu, a Vietnamese official. Settlements of the Cao Dai followers in South Vietnam are located near the church in Tay Ninh. The number of followers of this sect is estimated at two million. Although it is founded on Buddhism and Taoism, its priesthood is patterned after that of the Catholic church.

Hoa Haoism was first introduced to Vietnam in 1939, founded by Huynh Phu So, a young monk. He advocated private prayer at home rather than in pagodas. More than one million Vietnamese are followers of this sect, many of them living in the western part of South Vietnam.

Culture

'Culture' in Vietnam spans a huge range of subjects, from its artistic heritage and traditional arts to its way of life. We will look at the most important of each of these in this chapter.

Architecture

Successive wars, both ancient and modern, have taken their toll on the architecture of Vietnam. Some buildings have survived and others are being restored, but overall little remains of the various civilisations that have ruled the country. In addition, renovation of ancient pagodas and temples has made little attempt to remain loyal to the original designs, with the result that modern elements have been introduced, even if they are inconsistent with the traditional styles.

The first of the three main civilisations in Vietnamese history was the Dong Son bronze-age civilisation, ruling from the 7th to the 2nd centuries BC, which covered a vast area from southern China to the coasts of Indonesia. During this era the Cham empire used mainly brick and clay to produce sculptures in honour of the Champa gods and kings, with masonry skills, especially in constructing graceful brick towers, that were highly advanced for the period.

From the 11th century, Vietnamese kingdoms started using carved wood to decorate temples and palaces. Much of the wood used in constructions and carvings has suffered in the tropical climate, although thankfully some examples have survived. Many temples or mausoleums, particularly around Hué, have survived because of the Vietnamese custom of ancestor worship, which has maintained these buildings in good condition.

Vietnamese architecture has also tended to be temporary. Buildings were often made of wood rather than brick, with the structure supported by columns rather than walls. Structures were built so that they could be dismantled and rebuilt elsewhere in times of natural catastrophe or a change in power. For example, in 1833 Emperor Minh Mang moved his throne at the Imperial City, Hué, so that he could build a huge palace in its place.

Art

The earliest examples of Vietnamese art date from the Don Son civilisation from the 7th century BC, when metalworking reached a high level of sophistication. Bronze objects such as drums, swords and lances are exquisitely carved, showing animals, hunting scenes or geometric patterns.

Cham art emerged around the 1st century, heavily influenced by India, especially the worship of the Hindu pantheon of gods, but it was only in the 15th century that it reached a high level of development. There are superb examples of ornamental and figurative sculpture at the Cham Towers at My Son, and at the Cham Museum in Danang.

Vietnamese art for a large part of its history has tended to be overshadowed by its great neighbour, China. Vietnam has tended to assimilate the art of other cultures, especially in periods of occupation and colonialism. For example, works of art between 1860 and 1945 tended to reproduce French colonial style.

One of the great artistic traditions of Vietnam, dating from the 13th century, is painting on frame-mounted silk. Scholar-calligraphers specialised in silk painting, often inspired by nature. In the 15th century, lacquerware was introduced from China, and remains one of the best-known of Vietnamese crafts. Lacquer is resin extracted from the *cay son* tree and was originally used to make wooden objects watertight, but later decorative uses were found. Up to ten coats of lacquer are applied successively, with a week's drying period between each coat.

It was only really in 1926, with the creation of the Indochinese School of Fine Arts, that Vietnamese artists discovered a freedom of expression unrestricted by the state or patronage. Now, there are many Vietnamese artists, some of whom exhibit abroad, but many who earn a living by reproducing famous Western paintings.

Culture

The Cham Towers of Phu Hai, Phan Thiet

Dress

The most famous of Vietnam's costumes is the traditional *ao dai* (pronounced 'ao zai' in the north and 'ao yai' in the south), worn by some schoolgirls, waitresses and shop assistants up and down the country. It has been admired by generations of men, both local and foreign, for it accentuates the woman's curves, yet retains its elegance and formality. It became the national costume in the 18th century upon the orders of Lord Nguyen. The long gowns are carefully tailored with three layers; two long slits along the side allow the gown to have two free-floating panels in the front and at the back of the dress, exposing a long pair of white silk trousers. Another classic Vietnamese item is the conical hat, made out of palm leaves. Some have poetry written on them (known as a *non bai tho*). This traditional hat is particularly suitable for a tropical country such as Vietnam, where fierce sunshine and hard rain are commonplace.

For formal ceremonies, men wear a long gown with slits on either side, and a turban, usually in black or brown made of cotton or silk. In feudal times there were strict dress codes. Ordinary people were not allowed to wear clothes with dyes other than black, brown or white. Costumes in yellow were reserved for the King. Those in purple and red were reserved for high-ranking court officials, while dresses in blue were worn by court officials.

Language

Vietnamese (Kinh) is the official language of the country, although there are dialectic differences across Vietnam. There are dozens of different languages spoken by various ethnic minorities, and Khmer and Laotian are spoken in some parts. The most widely spoken foreign languages in Vietnam are Chinese (Cantonese and Mandarin), English, French and Russian. Understandably, given Vietnam's recent past, the older

A traditional singer

generation are more likely to speak French as a second language, while middle-aged people are more likely to speak Russian or other Eastern European languages. The young have wholeheartedly embraced English, which is quickly becoming the unofficial second language.

Music

Vietnamese music has a long history. For the Vietnamese, music is considered to be an essential need, used for a number of purposes: to express their innermost feelings, for encouragement while working and fighting, to educate their children in good traditions and national sentiment, to communicate with the gods or spirits, and to express their aspirations for a happy life. The Vietnamese musical tradition includes folk songs, used at festivals, funerals, at work or for courtship; classical music, which is more formal and originated in the north of the country and from Hué, where it was performed for the emperor or mandarins; and music to accompany theatre performances.

Many of the ethnic minorities in Vietnam have their own musical traditions and distinctive instruments such as reed flutes or lithophones (similar to xylophones). Modern Vietnamese music is strongly Western-influenced, and many pop singers and bands are emerging. Vietnamese pop seems to have borrowed all the worst features of Western pop but with a

A variety of Mien silverware and clothing from Northern Vietnam

unique form of Vietnamese kitsch thrown in for good measure.

Theatre

Vietnamese theatre is varied, often using elements such as dance, mime, recitation, music and singing. Classical theatre is based on Chinese opera, with simple characterisation and acting. Make-up is used accordingly, for example with red face paint representing courage and loyalty. Popular theatre often uses satire as a form of social protest, with songs of peasant origin.

Water puppetry (*roi can*) is the most famous Vietnamese form of dramatic art and can be seen in its most authentic form in Hanoi. It is thought to have ancient origins in the Red River Delta (Northern Vietnam) as a form of entertainment during flooding in the wet season. It is performed in a pool of water with the surface acting as the stage.

Eating Vietnamese style

Eating plays an important part in Vietnamese society, with its own etiquette and customs. To immerse yourself in Vietnamese culture, it is essential to be aware of how locals eat.

Food etiquette

Here are some basic guidelines to eating in Vietnam:

The importance of rice It has always been the country's key foodstuff, in terms of the economy, culture and way of life, with virtually all meals revolving around rice. Wasting rice is frowned upon.

What to eat and when Breakfast normally consists of a noodle soup such as *pho* or a sticky rice cake. People usually go home for lunch or eat in street cafés near their work around 11am. Lunch consists of rice with vegetables and fish or meat, and soup. Family bonding takes place at dinner time, with a selection of dishes like those at lunch time.

Using chopsticks It is worth learning how to use chopsticks properly, although no one will be offended if you ask for a knife and fork. Don't try to balance food on your chopsticks while carrying from the table to your mouth. Instead, hold your bowl near your mouth and use the chopsticks to shovel the food in your mouth.

Sharing Dining is a communal affair. Order a selection of dishes to share. Take rice from the large shared dish and put it in your bowl, before using your chopsticks to take meat, fish or vegetables from the serving dishes. If you eat with locals, don't be surprised if they pick out the best-looking pieces of meat and put them in your bowl. This is a way of honouring you as a guest. When passing or taking something, always use both hands and acknowledge the transaction with a small nod.

The lowdown on *pho* Pronounced 'fur', it is essentially a clear noodle soup, usually with strips of beef, and many other ingredients such as bean sprouts, ginger and a variety of leaves

The popular *nem lui,* a Hué speciality

Vietnam's famous fish sauce fermenting next to Mui Ne's sand dunes

stalls often serve just one dish or display a limited selection of dishes. The most common foods available on the street are:

Pho: noodle soup, often with beef (*bo*).

Xoi: a mixture of sticky rice, beans, fresh peanuts and pork, rolled in a banana leaf and steamed.

Chao: ground rice cooked slowly with pieces of meat, served with coriander leaves and chives.

Nem (north) or **Goi cuon** (south): rice paper pancakes, with a stuffing mixture of white meat, vermicelli, bean sprouts, black mushrooms and shrimps.

Banh cuon: Vietnamese ravioli, stuffed with minced pork, shrimps and mushrooms, then steamed.

Bun bo: Vermicelli with fresh herbs, beef and ground peanuts.

such as coriander, mint and basil. You can add chilli sauce, lime juice and fish sauce to your taste. *Pho* is revered in Vietnam, for it is both hearty and delicate, simple yet complex. It is eaten for breakfast or lunch in both street-side stalls and expensive restaurants.

Street food

Food on the street is healthy, cheap and delicious. Because it is made fresh, it is more hygienic than in some restaurants where food is left lying around. Street kitchens with little plastic tables and chairs are good places to mix with the locals. Street

FISH SAUCE

Fermented fish sauce or *nuoc-mam* plays the role of salt in Vietnamese meals. It is made using a cocktail of phosphorus and nitrogen, fermented in a long process. Layers of fish and salt are left to marinate and ferment for three months; then the bottom layer of liquid is drawn off and the remainder left to ferment for another three months. The best fish sauce comes from Phan Thiet and Phu Quoc Island. There are *nuoc-mam* connoisseurs who can judge which sauces have improved best with age and which has the richest flavours. In the north, fish sauce is used on its own as a dip for food such as spring rolls, whereas in the south it is mixed with garlic, sliced chilli and lime juice.

Festivals and events

Festivals are an important cultural activity of the Vietnamese people. They are attractive to all social classes and have been a necessary part of people's lives for many centuries. Festivals are the crystallisation of cultural, spiritual and physical activities, maintained over many generations. Most Vietnamese festivals are fixed by the lunar calendar: the majority take place in spring, and the days of the full moon (day one) and the new moon (day fourteen or fifteen) are particularly auspicious. All Vietnamese calendars show both the lunar and solar (Gregorian) months and dates. When the moon is full, special prayers are held at pagodas. Many Buddhists eat only vegetarian food on these days.

A beautifully clad girl during Tet celebrations

Tet

Tet Nguyen Dan, or simply Tet ('festival'), is Vietnam's most important annual event; it lasts for seven days and falls sometime between the last week of January and the third week of February, on the night of the new moon. This is a time when families get together to celebrate renewal and hope for the new year, when ancestral spirits are welcomed back to the household, and when everyone in Vietnam becomes a year older – age is reckoned by the new year and not by individual birthdays. Everyone cleans their house from top to bottom, pays off debts, and makes offerings to Ong Tau, the Taoist god of the hearth. The eve of Tet explodes with a cacophony of drums and percussion and the following week is marked by feasting on special foods. For tourists,

Tet can be a great time to visit Vietnam, but it pays to remember that most of Vietnam, including transport services, closes down during this period and for the week after the new year.

Other national festivals

Holiday of the Dead (Thanh Minh) in April commemorates deceased relatives.

Tiet Doan Ngo (Summer Solstice Day) in June sees the burning of human effigies to satisfy the need for souls to serve in the God of Death's army.

Wandering Souls Day (Trung Nguyen), held on the fifteenth day of the seventh moon (August), is the second-largest festival of the year, when offerings of food and gifts are given to the wandering souls of the forgotten dead.

Trung Thu is also known as Children's Day, when dragon dances take place and children are given lanterns in the shape of stars, carp or dragons (September–October).

Regional festivals

Festivals in specific parts of the country that may interest tourists include:

The Water Puppet Festival held at Thay Pagoda, west of Hanoi (February).

The two-week Buddhist full moon festival at the Perfume Pagoda, west of Hanoi (March–April).

Festivals and events

Tet celebrants at Tran Quoc Pagoda, Hanoi

People

Vietnam has the second-largest population in Southeast Asia, with around 84 million inhabitants, and it is growing fast. For an agricultural country Vietnam has a high population density, especially in the Red River and Mekong deltas, which account for 40 per cent of the country's population. This has lead to Viet people settling in less inhabited areas such as the Highlands, traditionally the domain of hill-tribe minorities.

The population

Vietnam is still a mainly rural country, with only 20 per cent of the population living in the cities, the biggest being Ho Chi Minh City with 6.2 million inhabitants and Hanoi with 3.2 million.

The government is trying to reduce population growth by punishing families who have more than two children, for example by denying the third child household registration, and by promising additional benefits in education and healthcare to families that keep to the limit.

Ethnic groups

There are five main ethnic 'families' in Vietnam, with 54 ethnic groups in total. The Kinh (or Viet) people account for 85 per cent of Vietnam's total population. Major ethnic minority groups include the Tay, Thai, Muong, H'mong, Dao and Khmer. There are ethnic Chinese (two per cent), and remnants of the Indianised Champa Kingdom, the Chams. There are also many other smaller ethno-linguistic groups known by the French term Montagnards (highlanders), which have developed their own language and cultural identity, living mainly in the Central Highlands.

Many ethnic minority groups can be visited in the mountains to the far north of the country, especially around Sapa, or the central highlands around Buon Ma Thuot, Kon Tum and Pleiku. In the past, ethnic groups in general have been sidelined politically and socially within Vietnam, but this is changing as tourism grows and the hill-tribes become recognised as attractions for visitors.

Austro-Asians

This 'East-Asian' family represents 94 per cent of Vietnam's population, comprising two language groups, the Viet-Muong and Mon-Khmer. The Viet and the Muong were both pioneers of northern Vietnam, the Viet originating in the Red River Delta and then moving southwards, giving up their traditional customs and maintaining their Chinese-influenced culture. The Muong, on the other hand, remained around the foothills of Hoa Binh, maintaining their traditional skills such as basket-weaving and using bamboo hydraulic systems to build canals. The Mon-Khmer group makes up 2 per cent of Vietnam's people and is dominated by the Khmers, who live in the Mekong Delta, descendants of the Angkor Empire (9th–15th centuries). Other Mon-Khmer groups are scattered about the Highlands, the most notable being the Ba Na from the Buon Ma Thuot region, famous for their grand stilt houses.

Tai-Kadai
This family makes up 3.7 per cent of the population, and is dominated by the Tai, who originally migrated from China, bringing with them customs such as house-building using clay, straw and unbaked bricks. They are known for their weaving, wood-carving and irrigation, and live mainly in the northwest. The Black Tai can be easily recognised, particularly at Son La, by a dark-indigo scarf wrapped around the head, displaying one of its triangular embroidered edges.

H'mong-Yao
Making up just 1.1 per cent of Vietnam's people, this group consists of traditionally nomadic peasants who rely on the natural resources of the mountains for their survival. The H'mong live in very basic dwellings in high regions, breeding horses, putting their blacksmith skills to valuable use, and organising fairs for both trade and social purposes. The Black H'mong from Sapa wear dark indigo costumes with stunning silver jewellery, often with their calves wrapped in indigo material. Red H'mong wear scarlet wool in their turbans, while Multicoloured H'mong wear brightly coloured material of batik and printed patterns.

The Yao (more commonly known as 'Dao', but pronounced 'Zao') are scattered in remote small villages, growing corn, fruit trees and medicinal plants. They are famous for their embroidery, using designs passed down from mother to daughter. Red Dao wear red pom-poms round their necks with red headdresses over a shaved forehead, while the Black Dao wear a variety of costumes, most commonly a long indigo panelled jacket over a batik skirt.

Children have fun at a fountain in Hanoi

Conduct and social etiquette

It is important that visitors to Vietnam understand and respect the cultural differences that they will encounter in the country.

Influences on society Traditional values are based on Confucian ideals, such as respect for the old, the worship of ancestors, the importance of the community over the individual, respect for custom and tradition, keeping one's word and the importance of education.

The north of the country is more imbued with Communist ideals and strong traditional values, while the south, especially the cities, has been influenced by Western attitudes to commerce and individuality. Rural areas continue to maintain a hierarchical society, while this is less prevalent in the towns. The opening up of the country to foreign ideas has created tension between the young and the old, with many children embracing Western activities such as e-mail chat-rooms, mobile phones and pop music.

Elements of traditional culture
The main cultural differences that tourists will encounter in Vietnam can be summarised into several key themes:

Smile A simple smile when communicating with locals works wonders for most situations. Vietnamese are mostly helpful, genuine people and they will bend over backwards to assist those that treat them with respect and friendship. Vietnamese people have a good sense of humour and fun, especially in the south, where people tend to be more openly friendly.

Saving face Vietnamese find it incredibly important to save face in all situations. Any show of anger is a definite no-no. When negotiating, do not grind the poor seller into the ground, show some respect and negotiate graciously. Never humiliate a Vietnamese when complaining about something, as this brings shame onto both you and them.

Pale is better You will notice that women cover their arms and even face when out in the sun. This is because pale skin is highly prized. Historically, tanned women were those who worked in the field and were therefore of a lower class.

Attitudes to marriage Vietnamese love family life, and see marriage as something that should be done as soon as possible, although modern thinking is denting this somewhat. They tend to pity someone who is still single or divorced, and find it strange

Local vendor in a conical hat

geomancers to placate spirits or create a better environment.

Privacy and personal space The Vietnamese do not share Western concepts of privacy, so bear this in mind when you are changing or using the bathroom. Similarly, don't be surprised if locals invade your personal space. Waiting to be served can be frustrating, as the Vietnamese do not understand queuing.

Centre of attention If you are in a rural area or away from tourist centres, do not be surprised if you become the centre of attention. You may get befriended by children eager to practise their English, while curious bystanders will gather round to observe. Showing photo prints of your home and family, or showing snaps on a digital camera display, are sure-fire ways to become popular.

Feet and shoes It is usual to take shoes off when entering someone's home, and is the norm when entering a Buddhist temple. It is considered rude to point the bottom of your feet towards people or anything sacred, especially when sitting on the floor.

that someone should be unmarried out of choice. Many Vietnamese will enquire about your marital status early on in a conversation. If you are single, it is best to reply 'not yet married.'

Women in society Confucian tradition dictates that women must submit to their husbands. However, below the surface, women exert a strong influence on the home, and especially in bringing up children. Many guesthouses, shops and restaurants are run by women.

Feng shui Known as *phong thuy* in Vietnam, geomancy is the art of manipulating or judging the environment. Ancestors' tombs, family altars and buildings are all constructed with geomantic principles in mind. Failing businesses have been known to call in

In general, Vietnam shares the same attitudes to dress and social taboos as other Southeast Asian cultures. In a pagoda or temple you are also expected to leave a small donation. Passing round cigarettes (to men only) is always appreciated.

Impressions

The first couple of days in Vietnam are filled with some degree of culture shock for many visitors, especially those from the Western world where order, structure and individuality are taken for granted. Landing in either Ho Chi Minh City or Hanoi and being driven from the airport to the city is going to be an experience. The streets will be clogged with motorbikes, bicycles and other vehicles and the constant honking of horns and the sheer mass of people is intimidating.

Culture shock

How can so many people live together in such close proximity and apparent harmony? You will find the answer to this as you spend more time in Vietnam and see Vietnamese virtues of patience, co-operation, family pride and selflessness at work in everyday life.

Traditional customs and values still exert a strong hold over Vietnamese culture, even if these are being eroded over the years by greater exposure to the West. For a start, traditional Vietnamese do not tend to pursue their ambitions as individuals, but rather as families, groups or communities. Villagers from the countryside tend to view their land not as their own, but as something that they are looking after during their lifetime, to be passed on to the next generation when the time comes. Ancestors are revered and remembered, with family shrines in most households in Vietnam. In the past, Vietnamese children would not talk about themselves as 'I', but according to who they were talking to, for example, when talking to their father, they would refer to themselves as 'Your son'. There is a strong family unity and community spirit that exists in the country. For example, neighbouring shopkeepers will look after each other, changing money, loaning stock, tending each other's stores. Businesses will be run by a complex network of family ties, friends and neighbours, co-operating effortlessly with each other.

You will notice that wherever you go, there will be many people involved in daily transactions. Any communication that you have with a local is likely to be observed, and talked about by family, neighbours and bystanders. Any shared moment of laughter you have with a Vietnamese will be amplified as they share the joke with anyone close enough to listen. Their innate curiosity towards foreigners is born from many years of isolation under Communist rule, and they are enjoying their new-found openness to the outside world.

As you become more comfortable in the crowded streets, you will begin to recognise newly arrived tourists, as they stand on the pavement, afraid to cross the street in front of a constant stream of motorbikes. This scenario symbolises what it is to adapt to Vietnamese life. The trick is to start crossing the road, taking care to walk slowly at a consistent pace. You will notice that motorbikes automatically steer out of your way, to the point that you don't really need to look at the oncoming traffic. As soon as you put your trust in others with something as trivial as crossing the road, you immediately realise that you are adapting to your new environment.

What to do and see

The first thing to emphasise is that Vietnam is a large country (1,650km/ 1,025 miles in length), so adapt your plans accordingly. The biggest mistake that tourists make is to plan to do too much, to see too many sights, to pack too much into their schedule. The minimum time recommended to see the highlights of the whole country is three weeks. You can do it in two, but you will need to pick your highlights carefully. The worst thing to do is to see too much and to be too exhausted to enjoy it.

It is fair to say that the north of Vietnam contains more highlights than the south. With only two weeks, you should focus on one or the other. For example, you can cover the north by visiting Hanoi, Sapa, Halong Bay, Hué

Landscape near Sapa

and perhaps Hoi An, as long as you take an internal flight or sleeper train between Hanoi and Hué, to minimise travelling time. In the south of the country, the highlights include the Mekong Delta, Ho Chi Minh City and one of the beach resorts such as Nha Trang, Mui Ne or Phu Quoc Island.

Much also depends on your specific area of interest. There is much to see for a variety of tastes. For example, history and culture buffs will enjoy Hanoi, Hué and Hoi An, while nature-lovers should spend several days in the northwest mountains around Sapa as a priority, in the central highlands around Plei Ku and Kon Tum, or in the southern highlands around Buon Ma

Thuot and Dalat. Those interested in the Vietnam War (known here as the 'American War') will want to travel around the DMZ (Demilitarised Zone) in the middle of the country, as well as visit some of the fascinating war museums in Ho Chi Minh City and Hanoi. Beach or water-sports lovers should consider the three top resorts, according to their specific requirements: Nha Trang for busy beaches, great water-sports facilities, top diving and snorkelling and lively nightlife; Mui Ne for a quieter, chilled-out beach resort experience; and Phu Quoc Island for dazzling scenery, limited infrastructure, but fantastic diving and snorkelling.

Two elderly women visiting a pagoda near Dalat

When to go

The peak tourist season in Vietnam is the dry season, which runs roughly from November to March. This is generally the best time to visit. That said, the tropical monsoon climate affects the north and south of the country differently, so visitors will find that they need to make choices about when and where to go. The south is generally about 5°C (8°F) warmer than the north. The south is at its most pleasant from November to late April, before the heat of the summer becomes too oppressive. The north is warm and sunny from October to December, before the cold and rain of winter sets in. This is the best time to visit Halong Bay, one of the natural wonders of the world (*see p68*). From January to March, the winter weather is unpredictable and can dampen the experience of Halong Bay considerably. The north does not get too cold in the winter, generally staying above 15°C (59°F) in the daytime. In the centre of Vietnam there is generally more rainfall, especially in Hué from September to February. The best time to visit the centre is February to May.

Getting around

There is a range of transport options available to visitors, with generally good transport links around the country. Buses are very cheap and relatively quick, considering the long distances. Trains are slower and more expensive, but provide more of an experience.

Internal flights are widely available at a reasonable cost, although much more expensive than buses.

Owing to the long distances involved, many travellers with a reasonable budget choose to fly at least one leg of their visit, for example between Hanoi and Hué, or Danang and Nha Trang. This often saves almost a whole day on a bus, at a reasonable cost (US$60–95). Alternatively, the sleeper train between Hanoi, Hué and Ho Chi Minh City (the famous Reunification Express) is a popular option that gets booked up quickly.

For those on a budget, open-tour buses are highly popular. You can choose the distance you want to travel and the ticket allows you to hop on and off at your will. For example, the best-known operator, Sinh Café, offers an open-tour ticket between Hanoi and Ho Chi Minh City for US$25–45. However, some find that bus travel starts to pall, because of the sheer number of hours that it entails.

How to behave

The Vietnamese are welcoming and hospitable people, although they may appear reserved at first. A smile and a word or two of Vietnamese goes a long way in breaking the ice. *Xin chao* (pronounced 'Sin ciao'), meaning 'hello', and *com on* (thank you) are the minimum language requirements for getting some degree of respect from your Vietnamese hosts.

A family in Hué

There is some difference between the north and south. Vietnamese in the south tend to be warmer, more friendly and outgoing than their northern counterparts. Northerners are generally hard-working, traditional and more formal. However, virtually all Vietnamese share a curiosity and interest in foreigners, with no hint of animosity or resentment that one would expect towards Westerners, considering Vietnam's tragic modern history.

The Vietnamese value courtesy and respect highly (*see p32*). Any show of anger is considered to be very bad form. Losing face is seen as humiliating, and must be avoided at all costs.

The language

Most Vietnamese who work in the tourist industry will have some command of English, and indeed some tourists never have to deal with any local who doesn't understand English. However, it is enjoyable and recommended to learn at least a few words of Vietnamese, because you will be treated better as a result. You may encounter laughter or puzzlement upon trying to utter Vietnamese words, but it will open many doors and close none. (For a guide to useful words and phrases, *see pp180–81*.) Many visitors adapt their English vocabulary and pronunciation according to their audience. Many Vietnamese are keen to improve their English but will have had limited contact with foreigners, and will therefore struggle to understand if you speak quickly. If you find yourself in a situation where neither party speaks the other's language, there is a fail-safe

Po Nagar Cham Towers, Nha Trang

Cyclo on a street in Hanoi

fall-back position: soccer! Vietnamese men love watching European league football, which is often televised. Just exchanging names of famous football players will be sufficient to establish a connection and a rapport.

Annoyances

While Vietnam is essentially a safe and enjoyable country to visit, it is a fact of life that most tourists will encounter some annoying or frustrating situations. It is an economic reality that Westerners have a far higher level of income than the average Vietnamese. Tourists are therefore seen as incredibly rich. Only a very few Vietnamese are able to afford to travel outside of their country. While most locals are honest, there is a small but growing minority of people who try to extract as much money as possible from tourists. This is sadly the same all over the world.

This can happen in innumerable ways, to the extent that you will

eventually start to admire the ingenious methods that exist to rip tourists off. For example, some hotels choose to pass on the 10 per cent tax that the government imposes, something that most hotels do not do. Some taxi drivers try to make the tourist pay the toll fee on the way to or from the airport. Hotels or restaurants can often miscalculate the bill to an alarming degree. Anything from bottles of water, cans of drink to taxis can be overcharged. Motorbike and cyclo drivers can be the worst offenders, choosing to ignore any attempts at agreeing on a price beforehand. Some tourists find these experiences infuriating and choose to let it spoil their trip. This is a mistake. These experiences can be minimised by being street-wise, but at the end of the day, it is unlikely that you will leave the country without being overcharged at some point. However, the fact is that you are most likely to lose by a very small amount of money, which in the long run is no real disaster.

The government is trying very hard to crack down on these instances of overcharging, and, overall, the majority of Vietnamese are scrupulously honest. It would be a shame to treat everyone with suspicion. The best thing to do is to agree a price before every transaction and check what is included in the price. This will cut down on the scope for 'misunderstandings'.

Beyond this, Vietnam is a safe country, with serious crime being virtually nonexistent. Petty crime is on the increase, though, especially in big cities. Ho Chi Minh City is perhaps the worst city, with bag-snatchings and pickpocketing being reported in the shopping districts.

Lifestyle

Adapting to the Vietnamese way of life is one of the pleasures of visiting the country. Slowly you will start to understand how things work and fit in accordingly. For example, you may start

eating at small local restaurants or street kitchens, enjoying a steaming bowl of beef noodle soup, a delicious street snack, or fresh local beer at a *bia hoi*, sitting on low plastic seats along with the locals. Vietnamese are early to bed and early to rise, with the streets often deserted by 10pm. You can get up early to stroll in the nearby park, to see Vietnamese taking their morning exercise by doing tai chi, stretching or playing badminton. Immersing yourself in the street life is one of the most enjoyable ways of interacting with the locals. Young people will come up to you to try to practise their English, babies will stare at the strange foreigners while their mothers smile amusingly at you, hawkers will walk up to you with the usual opening 'Where you from?' and engage in some half-hearted banter. And everywhere, locals will not fail to respond to a smile with a grin and a nod of acknowledgement. When you leave, you will be full of memories, and if you are lucky, your soul will be richer for the experience.

Impressions

Friendly young locals in the Mekong Delta

Hanoi

Vietnam's small, elegant capital lies in the heart of the northern delta, known as the Red River Delta. It is one of the prettiest cities in Southeast Asia, a romantic yet bustling city that reflects its French and Chinese heritage. Given the political and historical importance of Hanoi and its growing population, fortunately it's a low-key city, unlike brash, young Ho Chi Minh City.

For those with limited time, Hanoi is the ideal base for visiting the cultural and natural wonders of Northern Vietnam, while there is much to enjoy in the city itself. There are museums aplenty, several districts to wander aimlessly in, soaking up the atmosphere. Although the traffic is a nuisance, as in most Vietnamese cities, it has a relatively relaxed feel to it, with plenty of cafés to while away the afternoon in, and restaurants of every type to satisfy a huge range of tastes.

The origins of the city date back 2,000 years. Present-day Hanoi (the name means 'Inside the Riverbend') was once a turtle and alligator-infested swamp with a cluster of villages made up of stilt houses. The villages were unified by Chinese administrators, who built ramparts around their headquarters and called the area 'Dominated Annam'. In the late 10th century the Vietnamese attained independence from the Chinese. King Ly Thai To made the city his capital in 1010 and gave it the name Thang Long ('Soaring Dragon').

According to legend, the King began rebuilding the former Chinese palace, but the walls tumbled down. While he prayed to the local earth god, a white horse emerged from the temple and the King decided to build his citadel walls along the traces of its hoof prints. The white horse is the city's guardian.

In the early 13th century guilds evolved from the collection of tiny workshop villages that clustered around the walled palace to satisfy the court's demand for the highest quality products. Artisan guilds worked and lived together, developing systems for transporting merchandise from the village of manufacture to the designated streets in the business quarter which sold it.

In 1887, the French turned Hanoi into the centre of government for the entire Union of Indochina, replacing ancient monuments with grand colonial residences, many of which survive today. Hanoi finally became the capital of independent Vietnam in 1954, with Ho Chi Minh its first president. The city sustained serious damage in the 'American War'. In fact, the Vietnamese believed Hanoi would be flattened by systematic American bombing and had prepared architectural plans for construction of a new capital.

The current city has surprisingly preserved itself well since the 1950s, due mainly to political isolation and a lack of resources for development. However, since the advent of tourism in 1993, it has seen an explosion in

Central Hanoi

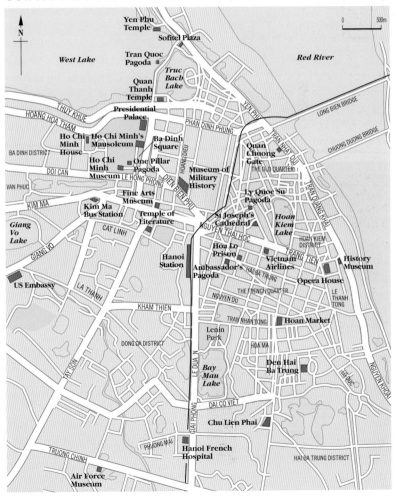

travellers' cafés, mini-hotels and internet cafés. There is a danger that the old charm of the city will be lost by frenetic development and construction. To counter this, the city government is working with international bodies to preserve the city's heritage.

HOAN KIEM DISTRICT

Hoan Kiem Lake is the soul of the city, as well as the epicentre of all the hustle and bustle in Hanoi. It is the most identifiable geographical landmark, sitting in the heart of the commercial centre of the city. To the north are the narrow streets and budget hotels of the Old Quarter, to the northwest are the grand monuments grouped around Ba Dinh Square, while to the south lie the grand avenues and colonial buildings of the French Quarter.

Hoan Kiem Lake

The lake offers respite and tranquillity from the rigours of sightseeing, and locals and visitors alike sit on the many park benches ringing the lake to gaze at the mirror-like expanse of water. There are several cafés around the north edge of the lake in which to enjoy a drink or ice cream while admiring the scenery. The lake comes alive early each morning, when locals come from all around to jog, exercise and practise their tai chi before the onslaught of the working day.

Temple of the Jade Mound (Den Ngoc Son)

A stuffed giant turtle, similar to the one in the famous legend, is housed here. It was captured in 1968 and is over 2m (6ft) long. The temple itself is accessed via the famous Huc Bridge, an arch of red-lacquered wood, described as 'the place where morning sunlight rests'.

This small temple was founded in the 14th century and is dedicated to a variety of historical celebrities. General Tran Hung Dao defeated the Mongols in 1288 and sits on the principal altar. The other personalities are Van Xuong, God of Literature; physician La To; and Quan Vu, a martial arts expert. The temple building is typical of the Nguyen dynasty, dating from the 1800s.

Thap Rua (Tortoise Tower), Hoan Kiem Lake

Tortoise Tower (Thap Rua)

This three-tiered pavilion is unmissable, sitting as it does on a tiny island in the centre of the lake. The literal translation of Ho Hoan Kiem is 'Lake of the Restored Sword', after a popular legend. Le Loi, a Vietnamese hero of the 15th century, led a successful uprising against the Chinese. He had found a sword while fishing in the lake ten years earlier and was preparing to thank the spirit of the lake for his victories when the sword flew out of its scabbard into the mouth of a golden turtle, sent by the gods to reclaim the weapon.

Water Puppet Theatre

Almost opposite the Huc Bridge is the Water Puppet Theatre, where tickets can be purchased during the day. Performances take place in water (the surface being the 'stage'). It is well worth buying the best seats possible, because the view is much better the nearer you get to the front. However, people in the front seats have been known to get splashed! The performance lasts 40 minutes, which is just about right.

St Joseph's Cathedral

To the west of the lake, past the upmarket souvenir shops in Nha To (Big Church) street, is this imposing neo-Gothic cathedral. Constructed in the 1880s, it has a grand high-vaulted interior, ornate altar screen, and stained glass windows. The last cardinal of Vietnam was buried in the black marble tomb in 1990. Over the tomb are several statues commemorating martyred Vietnamese saints, such as André Duc Lac, executed in 1839 on the orders of the anti-Christian Emperor Minh Mang.

Nha To. Entrance is via a small door in the southwest corner, except during services when the main door is open. Admission free.

Ly Quoc Su Pagoda

To the north of the cathedral along Ly Quoc Su is this small pagoda bearing the same name, housing an interesting collection of statues. Dating from the 12th century, it is named after a Buddhist royal advisor to King Ly Than Tong, Ly Quoc Su (also referred to as Minh Khong). His claim to fame is that he cured the King of the hallucination that he was a tiger. Ly Quoc Su's image lies on the principal altar, next to the white-bearded Tu Dao Hanh.

50 Ly Quoc Su, west of Hoan Kiem Lake. Open: daily.

HIGHLIGHTS OF HANOI

While there is much in the city, the key things to do are:
• take a cyclo tour around the city centre
• visit the wonderful Temple of Literature
• pop in to see 'Uncle Ho' at the Ho Chi Minh Mausoleum
• stroll around the bustling streets of the Old Quarter
• get up early and join the locals exercising on the banks of Hoan Kiem Lake
• sip strong Vietnamese coffee in one of the many cafés in the elegant French Quarter.

Walk: Around Hoan Kiem Lake

This walk covers some of the best-known sights in central Hanoi, with Hoan Kiem Lake as the focal point. It is a good stroll to take early on in your trip, so that you can get your bearings in this atmospheric, fascinating city.

Allow 2 hours (plus time in places of interest and food and drink stops).

Start at the north end of Hoan Kiem Lake. The red Hué Bridge is unmissable, and an ideal place to start the walk.

1 Hué Bridge

This bridge is the subject of countless tourist postcards. Beside the bridge stands the Writing Brush Tower, an obelisk 9m (30ft) high. On it, three outsized Chinese characters proclaim 'a pen to write on the blue sky'.
Walk over the bridge to the island.

2 Temple of the Jade Mound

Den Ngoc Son, as it is known in Vietnamese, is a small temple sheltering among ancient trees (*see p44*). For some, the highlight of this temple is the rather ugly stuffed giant turtle similar to the one that starred in the famous legend of the lake.
Cross back over the bridge. Almost opposite is the Water Puppet Theatre, which you are sure to visit one evening during your stay. Turn left and walk around the north edge of the lake, taking
the northward-running Luong Van Can. Second on the left is Hang Gai. Take this street heading west, and take the second turning in the left, Ly Quoc Su, heading south. You will see the pagoda at No 50.

3 Ly Quoc Su Pagoda

This small pagoda (*see p45*) is famous for its distinctive statues, including Ly Quoc Su, a royal advisor who cured the King of his hallucinations.

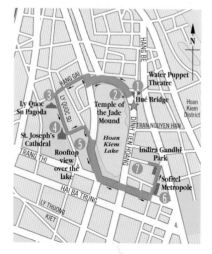

Head south along Ly Quoc Su and you will not fail to see the cathedral on the right. Outside the hours of Mass, the entrance is a door at the southwest corner.

4 St Joseph's Cathedral

The most interesting points in this French-built cathedral are the stained-glass windows and the high vaulted interior. Although the exterior is weathered, it cuts an imposing figure at the end of Nha Tho (Big Church) street.

The Sofitel Metropole Hanoi

Continue east and turn right onto Hang Trong, which takes you to Le Thai To and the southwest corner of the lake. At 38 Le Thai To, walk through the car park and find the lift near the rear of the building, going to the 6th floor.

5 Rooftop view over the lake

It is well worth seeking out Highlands Coffee here for its unbeatable views over the lake.

Cross the road to the south edge of the lake, and walk through the park, heading eastwards and continuing along Hang Khay which becomes Trang Tien. You will see the stunning Opera House in the distance. Turn left onto Ngo Quyen, and look out for an impressive white colonial building on your right at No 15.

6 Sofitel Metropole

This is one of Southeast Asia's great hotels, and an historic institution in its own right. It is worth walking round the old section of the hotel to admire the quintessentially French colonial atmosphere and sumptuous décor. If you can't afford to stay here, just visit for a drink at one of the elegant bars, and imagine!

Continue along Ngo Quyen, turning left into Le Thach. On this corner is the Governor of Tonkin's Residence, one of the city's most attractive colonial buildings, built in 1918. There is no entry to the public.

7 Indira Gandhi Park

This pleasant park runs alongside Le Thach, and is worth visiting later on in the afternoon. Families come here to play badminton on the courts marked out around the park. It is enjoyable to sit on a bench or the Indochinese-style bandstand to watch the locals at play. The park is known locally as Chi Linh, and was formerly known as Paul Bert Square, built during the development of the lakeside in 1886.

The west end of the park is opposite the lake. Facing the lake, the Post and Communications Building occupies the block to your left, a grand colonial-style building which houses the Post Office.

The 36 guilds

Hanoi's Old Quarter was originally arranged with each street selling one category of goods. Many of the street names represent the goods sold, such as Silver Street, Paper Street or Silk Street. This came from a village tradition of unity where craftsmen worked in the same trade and therefore the artisans' guilds (*phuongs*) make up what is known as the 36 Streets. Traditionally, the street engaged in both the production and the commercial sale of the goods.

A scene on Hang Duong (Sugar Street)

In the 18th century each street was the home of a particular craft guild, many of which were founded by members of the villages in the countryside surrounding Hanoi. Various plans are now being considered by the Hanoi People's Committee to limit traffic in the quarter.

Although the area is often called the 36 Old Streets, there may have actually been more. Some believe that the number 36 came from the 15th century, when there might have been 36 guilds. Others attribute the name '36' to a more abstract concept. The number 9 in Asia represents 'plenty'. Nine times 4 (the four directions) would make 36, which means 'many'.

Each guild had its own patron saint, to which many local temples are dedicated. Hang Bong Street has five such temples. A majority of the street names here start with Hang, which means 'merchandise' or 'shop'. The guild streets were named for their product or location. For example, skilled silversmiths from Hai Hung province now occupy Hang Bac Street, one of the most ancient streets in Vietnam, dating from the 13th century. Bac means silver, and appropriately, this street started as a

A scene on Hang Don (Copper Street)

silver ingot factory under the reign of Le Thanh Tong (1469–97).

Hang Ma and Hang Thiec are among the few streets in the quarter that have retained their ancient trades. Hang Ma sells colourful votive paper, 'ghost money' and other paper objects associated with the cult of the ancestors. The objects are burned in temples on the first and fifteenth days of the lunar month as offerings to the dead. Hang Thiec is the street of tinsmiths. The noise of hammers striking metal begins early in the morning and goes on late into the night. Vietnamese craftsmen extend an old tradition into modern times, fashioning a wide variety of kitchen utensils, boxes, and tanks for *bia hoi* (beer) and water, using relatively simple hand tools.

Ma May Street is a union of two old streets. Hang May sold rattan products, and Hang Ma sold sacred joss (paper replicas of money and of items such as clothing and even stereo sets) to burn for the dead. Ma is burned in front of the altar of ancestors accompanied by prayers. Around the turn of the 20th century, the streets became one: Ma May.

Other streets have changed their trade through the years. For example, Hang Duong (Sugar Street) now sells clothes. Hang Quat, which originally sold paper fans, is now lined with shops selling altar furnishings.

Here are some of the more well-known streets, their meanings and what they currently specialise in:
Hang Bo (Baskets), now haberdashers;
Hang Buom (Sails), now imported foods and alcohol;
Hang Chieu (Mats), mats, ropes, bamboo blinds;
Hang Dau (Oils), now shoes;
Hang Dieu (Pipes), now cushions and mattresses;
Hang Duong (Sugar), now clothes;
Hang Gai (Hemp), now silk, tailoring and souvenirs;
Hang Hom (Wooden chests), now glue, paint, varnish;
Hang Ma (Votive papers), paper goods;
Hang Quat (Fans), religious accessories;
Hang Thiec (Tin), tin goods, mirrors;
Hang Vai (Cloth), now bamboo ladders.

An altar at the Ngoc Son Temple

THE OLD QUARTER

If you only have time to do one thing in Hanoi, a stroll through the Old Quarter is a must. Known as Pho Co in Vietnamese, it is where the city's customs and traditions still live, 2,000 years on. If you are looking for the core, the essence, the heart of Hanoi, you will find it in Pho Co. Full of human activity, it still feels very much from a bygone era, before the days of shopping malls and retail chains. It is a square kilometre (^{1}/$_3$sq mile) of extremes – industry, elegance, dirt, chaos, and, above all, humanity.

The architecture is mainly from the 18th and 19th centuries, in addition to a jumble of new buildings. The streets are narrow and bustling, but not in an impersonal way. Commercial life buzzes around the streets, with goods being loaded and unloaded on the pavements, and an endless stream of motorbikes flowing through the junctions, and pedestrians walking gingerly in the gutter, avoiding the rows of parked motorbikes and displays of goods that crowd the pavement.

Commoners' homes evolved out of market stalls before streets ever came into existence. Because shops were taxed by the width of frontage on the market, storage and living space moved to the rear. They developed into the long and narrow houses, called tube houses. In general, the homes have a front room serving as the place where goods can be manufactured, followed by a small open courtyard to let in light, and a back room that is used as living quarters.

The streets are alive and bustling almost 24 hours a day. By 5.30am, people are out on the sidewalk exercising, washing clothes and playing badminton. Economic activity starts at 6am with restaurants opening for breakfast, shopkeepers getting ready for the day and street vendors arranging their wares. By 9pm the streets quieten down, as families spend the evening together eating and socialising.

87 Ma May

A beautiful example of a traditional tube house, this small museum was originally owned by Chinese traders.

It has been lovingly restored and is a delightful place to look around. The friendly staff are dressed in traditional *ao dai* costume and welcome you with tea and a tour of the premises.
87 Ma May. Tel: (04) 928 5604. Open: daily 8am–5.30pm. Admission charge.

Bach Ma Pagoda

This is the oldest and most revered place of worship in the district. It was founded in the 9th century and dedicated to Bach Ma, the White Horse that helped King Ly Thai To to resolve the problem of the citadel's collapsing walls, according to legend. The present structure dates back to the 18th century.
76 Hang Buom.
Open: daily 8–11.30am and 2–5.30pm. Admission free.

Huyen Thien Pagoda

Scattered throughout the Old Quarter are pagodas and temples such as the Huyen Thien Pagoda. These places of worship are quite active even today, and attended by people of all ages, especially during auspicious lunar days. Tourists may walk into the pagodas, and are welcome to take pictures.
54 Hang Khoai. Admission free.

Quan Chuong Gate

This is the only surviving example of the 16 gates of the fortified enclosure that surrounded the commercial quarter up to the 19th century. It dates from 1749, although the original city gates were built in 1010.
Junction of Hang Chieu and Quan Chuong.

A busy scene outside the Bach Ma Pagoda

A bronze of a North Vietnamese soldier, History Museum

THE FRENCH QUARTER

Situated to the south of Hoan Kiem Lake, this area is much more spaced out than many other parts of the city. The first concession to develop the city was granted in 1874 to the French, who established the administrative capital for their new protectorate of Indochina in this area of the city.

The main artery of the French Quarter is Trang Tien, which ends in front of the Opera House. Along this road you will find bookshops and art galleries, as well as the Trade Plaza and an incongruous supermarket.

The area south of Trang Tien was known as Ville Française. It was French Hanoi's residential enclave, consisting of a grid of shaded boulevards whose distinguished villas are now much sought-after for restoration as embassies, offices or expatriate residences. These houses run the gamut of early 20th-century French architecture from elegant neoclassical to 1930s Modernism and Art Deco, with an occasional Oriental flourish.

Ambassadors' Pagoda

Also known as Chua Quan Su Pagoda, this is one of Hanoi's most active pagodas. It was built in the 15th century in an area that was put aside to accommodate ambassadors visiting the city. A magnificent iron lamp hangs over the crowded prayer-floor and ranks of crimson-lacquered Buddhas glow through a haze of incense. Its long openwork walls are sculpted with stylised lotus flowers.

73 Quan Su, between Ly Thuong Kiet and Tran Hung Dao. Open: daily 7.30–11.30am and 1.30–5.30pm. Admission charge.

History Museum

Situated one block east of the Opera House and built in the 1930s by l'Ecole Française d'Extreme Orient, this building is a fanciful blend of Vietnamese palace and French Villa, which came to be called 'Neo-Vietnamese'. Inside, exhibits include arrowheads and bronze drums from the Dong Son culture. One of the highlights is an impressive collection of Cham statuary. Upstairs, there are eye-catching ink-washes depicting Hué's Imperial Court in the 1890s, along with sobering evidence of royal decadence and French colonial brutality.

1 Pham Ngu Lao. Tel: (04) 824 1384. Open: Tue–Sun 8.30–11.30am and 1.30–4.30pm. Admission charge.

Hoa Lo Prison

Built by the French to house nationalist leaders, the prison was used during the

American War to house captured US pilots, who nicknamed it the 'Hanoi Hilton'. It is now a museum, describing the ill-treatment of political prisoners by the French colonialists. There are a few grim cells which were still in use up to 1994, and also some instruments of torture from the French period.

1 Hoa Lo, at the crossroads of Tho Nuom and Ly Tuong Kiet. Open: Tue–Sun 8–11.30am and 1.30–4.30pm. Admission charge.

Museum of the Vietnamese Revolution

This museum catalogues the 'Vietnamese people's patriotic and revolutionary struggle' from the first anti-French movements of the late 19th century to post-1975 reconstruction. Much of the tale is told through original documents, including revolutionary documents penned by Ho Chi Minh. There is a small exhibition on the 'American War' (which is tackled in greater depth at the Museum of Military History, *see p60*).

216 Tran Quang Khai. Tel: (04) 825 4151. Open: Tue–Sun 8–11.30am and 1.30–4pm. Admission charge.

Opera House

A *belle époque* delight built in 1911, the Hanoi Opera House has only recently been restored to its former glory, complete with its preserved crystal chandeliers, Parisian mirrors and sweeping staircase of polished marble. It is now the Municipal

Theatre, based on the neo-Baroque Paris Opéra.

Sofitel Metropole

Once called 'the jewel of Hanoi', this hotel opened in 1901 as the Grand Metropole Palace, and is one of Southeast Asia's great hotels. In 1990, it was restored by the Pullman-Sofitel group and became the city's first international-class hotel. Its illustrious guest book includes Graham Greene, who came here in 1952, and Jane Fonda, who stayed while making her famous broadcast to American troops. Journalist Bernard Falls described the hotel during the 1950s as a place where the barman 'could produce a reasonable facsimile of almost any civilised drink except water'.

15 Ngo Quyen. Tel: (04) 826 6919.

The Opera House

AROUND BA DINH SQUARE

Ba Dinh Square is the nation's ceremonial epicentre. Around the vast open spaces of the square are dotted the most important sites and museums relating to the great leader Ho Chi Minh, father of Communist Vietnam; his mausoleum, house and museum are all located here.

The square is 2km (1^1/4 miles) northwest of Hoan Kiem Lake, about 30 minutes' walk, or a short ride by cyclos or *xe om* (motorbikes), which will bring you here from the centre for less than US$1 (be prepared to negotiate). It is decorated with 168 grass squares, symbolising the patchwork scenery of the country's rice plantations.

It was here that Ho Chi Minh read out the Declaration of Independence to half a million people on 2 September 1945. The vast rectangular esplanade was created in commemoration in 1970. Independence is celebrated in the square each National Day with military parades.

The square is now popular with locals, especially in the evening, as an area to stroll and relax in the fresh air, away from the crowded streets of the city. Every night at 9pm, the massive flag in the centre of the square is lowered by a contingent of white-uniformed soldiers, with much ceremonial gravitas. It is a sober, respectful occasion worth experiencing.

Ho Chi Minh Mausoleum

This is the city's most popular tourist attraction, with large queues of locals

forming each weekend to pay their respects to 'Uncle Ho'. The imposing grey structure dominates the square, in stark contrast to its contents: the frail, embalmed figure of Ho Chi Minh himself, dressed in faded khaki clothes and plain rubber shoes, displayed in a glass coffin. For some, a visit to see 'Uncle Ho' is a strangely moving experience, accentuated by the dark, cold room and sombre atmosphere.

The Mausoleum itself was built in 1973, on the foundations of the old rostrum in Ba Dinh Square where president Ho Chi Minh used to chair national meetings. Every year the mausoleum closes in October and November, while Ho is sent to Russia for his annual 'holiday', to undergo maintenance.

Open: summer Tue–Thur 7.30–11.30am, Sat, Sun & public holidays 7.30–11am; winter Tue–Thur 8–11am, Sat, Sun & public holidays 8–11.30am. Foreigners must sign in at an office at 8 Hung Vuong, south of the Mausoleum, then leave their cameras, bags and hats at another checkpoint. There are strict rules of behaviour in the building: no talking, no hands in pockets, no hats, shorts or vests.

Ho Chi Minh House

This attraction provides a fascinating insight into the personality and values of Ho Chi Minh. After independence in 1954 President Ho Chi Minh refused to live in the splendour of the French imperialist Presidential Palace, preferring the more modest comfort of

Ho Chi Minh Mausoleum

the gardener's house in the palace grounds. After a few years, he built a modest dwelling for himself behind the palace, modelling it on an ethnic minority stilt house. The ground-level meeting area was used by Ho and the politburo; upstairs, his study and bedroom are sparsely furnished and unostentatious. Small, built of fine lacquered and polished wood in 1958, it contains but two rooms: a study and a bedroom. A tour by knowledgeable guides is included in the ticket price.
Hung Vuong. Open: Tue–Thur, Sat, Sun 8–11am and 1.30–4.30pm.
Admission charge.

Ho Chi Minh Museum

This museum tries to illustrate Ho Chi Minh's life using innovative symbolic displays of socialist realism and Vietnamese mythology. The results are surreal and somewhat bizarre. However, there are some interesting archives and photographs. The museum was opened in 1990 on the 100th anniversary of Ho's birth.
3 Ngoc Ha, southwest of Ba Dinh Square. Open: Tue–Thur, Sat, Sun 8–11.30am and 2–4pm. Admission charge.

One Pillar Pagoda

This unique pagoda is a simple structure that rivals the Tortoise Tower in Hoan Kiem Lake as a symbol of Hanoi. It is supported on a single column rising from the middle of a lake, the whole structure designed to resemble a lotus blossom, the Buddhist symbol of purity. It was founded in the 11th century and reconstructed in 1954 after the French destroyed it when evacuating the city.

The temple commemorates the legend of Emperor Ly Thai Tong, the childless emperor who dreamed that the Buddhist goddess of mercy and compassion, seated on a lotus flower, handed him a baby boy. When he eventually had a son in 1049, he constructed the pagoda in appreciation. Steps away is Dien Huu Pagoda, a delightful temple enclosing a bonsai-filled courtyard.
Ong Ich Kiem, southwest corner of Ba Dinh Square. Open: daily 6am–6pm.

Presidential Palace

This ornate mustard-yellow-coloured palace, built in 1906, served as the living and working quarters of Indochina's governor-general. When Ho Chi Minh returned to Hanoi after the defeat of the French in 1954 he refused to live in the palace itself. Today the building is used for formal international receptions and other important government meetings. You can view the structure from the outside but cannot go in. Surrounding the building are extensive gardens and orchards, as well as the famed Mango Alley, the 90m (300ft) pathway from the palace to Ho Chi Minh's stilt house. *Hung Vuong S. and Hoang Van Thu, north end of Ba Dinh Square. No entry.*

AROUND THE TEMPLE OF LITERATURE

The area between Ba Dinh Square and the French Quarter is one full of fascinating places of interest. Many of the embassies are located along its wide avenues, and it contains a real mix of historical sights and museums. The Temple of Literature is the most famous sight in the area, attracting a stream of tour buses and backpackers who travel westwards from Hoan Kiem Lake on cyclos and *xe om* (motorbikes). Northeast of here is the old 19th-century citadel, which occupies a huge, walled space directly west of the Old Quarter. It is here that the Museum of Military History (also known as the Army Museum) is located.

Temple of Literature

One of the undoubted highlights of the city is this ancient seat of learning and Vietnam's principal Confucian sanctuary. It is a walled island of

An altar in the House of Ceremonies, the Temple of Literature

tranquillity, surrounded by noisy traffic-laden roads on all sides.

Also known as Van Mieu, it was Hanoi's first university, built in 1070 and modelled on the ground plan of Confucius' birthplace in Qufu, China. It is a sprawling complex of structures of past Confucian studies and contains five walled courtyards. The temple is one of the few remnants of the Ly kings' original 11th-century city.

The third courtyard contains the central Well of Heavenly Clarity (a walled pond), flanked by the temple's most valuable relics: 82 stone stelae mounted on tortoises. Each stele records the results of a state examination held at the National Academy between 1442 and 1779, and gives biographical details of successful candidates.

Passing into the fourth courtyard brings you to the ceremonial hall, a long, low building whose sweeping, tiled roof is crowned by two lithe dragons bracketing a full moon. Here the king and his mandarins would make sacrifices before the altar of Confucius. These days recitals of traditional music are held among the ironwood pillars. Directly behind the ceremonial hall lies the temple sanctuary, where Confucius sits with his four principal disciples. The fifth courtyard used to house the National Academy, Vietnam's first university, but was destroyed by French bombs in 1947.

66 Nguyen Thai Hoc. Tel: (04) 845 2917 or 823 5601. Open: daily summer

Museum of Military History

7.30am–5.30pm; winter 7.30am–5pm. Admission charge.

Fine Arts Museum

This three-storey colonial block houses an excellent collection of works devoted to the country's artistic heritage, including architecture, sculpture, drawing and fine arts. The central exhibition rooms on the first floor contain some of Vietnam's most stunning lacquer painting, much of it excellent examples of socialist realism and so-called combat art. The ground floor contains superb examples of Dong Son bronze sculptures, as well as

Continued on p60

Walk: Ba Dinh Square towards the Temple of Literature

The walk will help you to orientate yourself in this part of Hanoi. It includes the most important sights in and around Ba Dinh Square, taking you past the old Citadel and towards the Temple of Literature. The best time to do this walk is early in the morning in order to avoid the queues for the Ho Chi Minh Mausoleum.

Allow at least 3 hours to reach the Temple of Literature, which you can tackle after lunch. If you decide not to enter any of the museums, the walk could take 2 hours.

Start at the south end of Ba Dinh Square – remember to register at 8 Hung Vuong before going into the Ho Chi Minh Mausoleum (see p54).

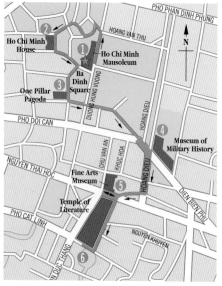

1 Ho Chi Minh Mausoleum

This most popular of Hanoi's sights is well worth queuing for. The reverence with which Ho Chi Minh is viewed is indicative of his importance in the history of Vietnam, as well as the values of its people.

Once you are back on Ba Dinh Square, walk north towards the Presidential Palace. Before reaching it, take the path to the left, past bamboo trees, where you will find the entrance to the Palace grounds and the ticket office to Ho Chi Minh's House.

2 Ho Chi Minh House

A guided tour of the compound will not take long. The atmosphere of the rooms, with their simple décor and furniture, is very personal. One can imagine Ho Chi

Minh sharing tea with Fidel Castro in the unassuming dining room in the former Gardener's House, discussing communist ideals and comparing notes!
The exit will bring you out very near the One Pillar Pagoda.

3 One Pillar Pagoda

This unusual pagoda with its tiny wooden sanctuary is one of the symbols of the city. Some people find its small scale and concrete pillar a bit of a letdown after the grandeur of the Mausoleum, but it is an important sight within Hanoi.
Walk westwards (away from Ho Chi Minh's Museum), and take Dien Bien Phu, a road lined with gnarled trees and colonial offices. Head southwest, aiming for the tall red-brick column on the edge of the old Citadel. Opposite a small park with a statue of Lenin is a white building on your left.

One Pillar Pagoda

4 Museum of Military History

This fascinating museum is full of photos, exhibits and old war weaponry. You can either go in or save the visit for another day.
As you exit this museum, follow Hoang Dieu southwards, past the flamboyant Chinese Embassy on your right, turning right on Cau Ba Quat to find a three-storey colonial block with brown shutters. Walk round to the south entrance, which is on Nguyen Thai Hoc.

5 Fine Arts Museum

Exhibits showing the country's artistic development are on show here. You can save the delights of this museum for another day, especially if you are in need of a rest!
Look southwards and you will see a walled compound with trees, which is the venerable Temple of Literature. Keep the compound on your right, and at 61 Van Mieu, you will find Koto restaurant, which is ideal for a spot of lunch. This well-run institution is staffed by former street kids who have been trained as part of a charity programme.

6 Temple of Literature

This gem of a sight is a relaxing way to end the tour. Stroll around the grounds and wonder at the beauty of the buildings and the high level of education achieved by the Ly kingdom in the 11th century.
From here you can easily find cyclos or xe om to take you back to your hotel, rather than face the ugly walk back to Hoan Kiem Lake or the French Quarter.

Walk: Ba Dinh Square towards the Temple of Literature

Ho Tay (West Lake)

Cham sculptures of dancing girls.
Examples of Ly Art (11th and 12th
centuries) and Tran Art (13th and 14th
centuries) are also included.
66 Nguyen Thai Hoc. Tel: (04) 823 3084.
Open: Tue–Sun 9am–5pm.
Admission charge.

Museum of Military History

Also known as the Army Museum, this
white, arcaded building can easily be
found, being situated at the foot of the
30m (100ft) high Cot Co Flag Tower, an
hexagonal tower built in the 1800s, one
of the few remnants of Emperor Gia
Long's citadel.

Lenin's statue still stands opposite the
museum, which supposedly traces the
story of the People's Army from its
foundation in 1944. However, the main

focus is on the French and American
Wars. Remnants of fighter planes, guns
and other weaponry are displayed in
the forecourt.
28a Dien Bien Phu. Tel: (04) 823 4264.
Open: Tue–Thur, Sat, Sun 8–11.30am
and 1–4pm. Admission charge.

THE WEST LAKE AREA

The West Lake is a shallow lagoon to
the north of Ba Dinh Square. It is one
of the most fashionable areas in the city
to live, with exclusive developments and
luxury hotels. It had humble
beginnings though, as a former holiday
resort for emperors, with summer
palaces and sponsored religious
foundations. The attractions of the lake
are grouped along the causeway
dividing the West Lake from Truc

Bac Lake. The nearest of these can easily be reached on foot, being just 500m (550 yds) north of the Presidential Palace.

Quan Thanh Temple

This 11th-century temple still stands on the lake's southeast bank, although it has been restored many times. It is dedicated to the Guardian of the North, Tran Vo, whose statue, cast in black bronze in 1677, is nearly 4m (13ft) high and weighs 4 tonnes. An important collection of 17th-century poems can be seen in the shrine room. Above the ornamented main gate is a 1677 replica of the bronze bell that supposedly lured the West Lake's legendary golden calf from China. Huge trees drape over the courtyard, keeping the temple and its environs cool and somewhat dark, even at midday.
Thanh Nien. Open: daily 8am–4.30pm. Admission charge.

Tran Quoc Pagoda

Hanoi's oldest temple dates from the 6th century, and is located on a tiny island on the West Lake. Originally, King Ly Nam De had a pagoda built on the bank of the Red River, which was moved to its current location more than 1,000 years later.

This modest temple is noted for its stele (inscribed stone slab) dating from 1639, which recounts the history of the pagoda and its move from the Red River, and the lovely brick *stupa* adjacent to the main temple. Tran Quoc is also an active monastery. In the main courtyard is a giant pink-and-green planter holding a bodhi tree, supposedly grown from a cutting from the original bodhi tree beneath which the Buddha reached his enlightenment.
Thanh Nien. Open: daily 7–11.30am and 1.30–6pm. Admission charge.

Boats and restaurant on Ho Tay (West Lake)

Hanoi environs and excursions

It is a shame that many tourists to Vietnam do not have the time to base themselves in Hanoi for longer. Often they have a couple of days in the city itself, before taking a tour to Sapa or Halong Bay, or heading southwards to Hué. For those with more time there is much to see in this area, either just out of Hanoi or a day-tour away. Getting out of the city gives you an alternative view of northern Vietnam and the richness of the landscape and history.

HANOI ENVIRONS

There are several sights worth visiting just a stone's throw from the city centre. Chief amongst these is the fabulous Museum of Ethnology, just on the outskirts of the city. If you have time, a visit to some of the beautiful temples around Hanoi is recommended. To the west are the Thay and Tay Phuong Pagodas, which can be visited together, and to the east the But Thap Pagoda, which can be visited in combination with other lesser temples in the area.

Museum of Ethnology

This huge museum on the western outskirts of the city has a dizzying array of artefacts from all over Vietnam, exhibiting the traditional cultures of Vietnam's ethnic groups. It is well worth the effort, with enough of interest in its exhibits and surrounding land to keep you occupied for several hours. Anyone who is considering venturing into the mountains to visit hill-tribe villages will find the museum an essential introduction to ethnic minorities. The French-designed, space-age building was built in 1986, and opened to the public in 1997. It has a high standard of exhibits with descriptions in French, English and Vietnamese, and videos and recreated village scenes that simulate life in the provinces. It is both a research centre and a public museum preserving the unique cultural identities of every ethnic group in the country.

The open-air section is particularly enjoyable. The peaceful grounds display different house styles, such as Ede long house, Tay stilt house, H'mong house with its *pomu* wood roof, the Viet tiled-roofed house, and even a Giarai tomb.

A craft shop outside sells books, bags and other items from various ethnic communities at reasonable prices.
Nguyen Van Huyen Road, Nghia Do, Cau Giay district. Tel: (04) 756 2193. Open: Tue–Sun 8.30am–5.30pm.

6km (4 miles) west of Hanoi. To get there, take a taxi or motorbike and follow Thuy Khue Avenue along the southern edge of the West Lake, and keep heading west. It is signposted left off Hoang Quoc Viet. Admission charge.

Thay Pagoda (The Master's Pagoda)

This attractive pagoda complex, also known as Thien Phuc Tu, is set next to a village and a pretty lake. While not a popular tour destination, it is well worth the visit in a private car or motorbike.

It was founded in the 11th century and dedicated to the monk Tu Dao Hanh, who performed miracles and was an accomplished water puppeteer (hence the theatre-pavilion in the middle of the lake – during the pagoda's annual festival, the lake is used for water-puppet shows). Tu Dao Hanh was said to have been reincarnated

Hanoi environs

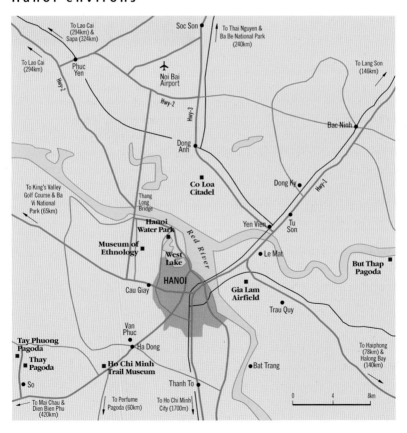

three times, as monk, Buddha and king, the last in response to the prayers of King Ly Than Tong for an heir.

Although the pagoda has been restored many times, the dark interior is still atmospheric, containing nearly 100 statues in the prayer halls. Most stunning are the two giant clay guardians from the 17th century, said to be the biggest in Vietnam.

In front of the pagoda are two covered bridges built in 1602, dedicated to the Sun and the Moon. There are steps up the hill, leading to sanctuaries, which Tu Dao Hanh is said to have climbed in order to die. From the top are fine views of the surrounding fields. You are likely to be accompanied up the steps by a local souvenir seller, offering to be your 'tour guide', who will expect payment of some sort.

30km (19 miles) from Hanoi, in Sai Son Village, between Ha Dong and Son Tay. Take Highway 6, turning right onto the TL72/TL80 to Quoc Oai, and carrying on for 4km (2¹/₂ miles) bearing right. Admission charge.

Tay Phuong Pagoda

Also known as 'The Pagoda of the West', this structure is composed of three parallel buildings on a small limestone hill. The 200-odd steps up the hill have been almost worn away over the years. The highlight here is the 76 figures exquisitely carved from jackfruit wood, amazingly lifelike representations of Buddhist ascetics as imagined by 18th-century sculptors.

A lacquered pillar in the Thien Chu Pagoda, Perfume Pagoda area

There are more of these figures in Hanoi's Fine Arts Museum.

The site dates back to the early 8th century, and is also an important Confucian sanctuary. The heavy double roofs, decorated with phoenixes and dragons, are another stunning feature of the pagoda.

40km (25 miles) southwest of Hanoi. A visit here is often combined with a visit to the Thay Pagoda, which is only 6km (4 miles) to the west. Admission charge.

But Thap Pagoda

A ride to But Thap, alternatively dubbed 'Two Dead Monks Pagoda', provides a superb afternoon outing for visitors keen to see a bit of countryside and desperate for some peace and quiet after the noise of Hanoi.

This tranquil 700-year-old temple, set amidst brilliant green rice paddies and hemp fields, is unknown to many travellers. But Thap Pagoda is strong on atmosphere, with amazing sculptures. Unlike that of other pagodas in Hanoi, the renovation of But Thap (as recently as 1992) has preserved the original look and feel of the pagoda, unspoiled by layers of lacquer and paint.

25km (16 miles) east from Hanoi, easily reached by Highways 1 or 5. The pagoda is due east from Le Mat, 'the snake village'. Tour offices do not usually get sufficient demand from travellers to see this temple, so you may find yourself organising a private tour. Alternatively, find a taxi that will take you, but negotiate first. Admission charge.

EXCURSIONS FROM HANOI

Among the various day-tours offered by Hanoi tourist offices, perhaps the most popular is the one to the Perfume Pagoda. It gets mixed reviews from tourists, although overall it does provide a fun day out of the city. Tam Coc's lovely scenery attracts many visitors who do not have time to visit Halong Bay, while Hoa Lu is an agreeable add-on to many Tam Coc tours.

Perfume Pagoda

The Perfume Pagoda (Chua Huong) is in fact a vast complex of pagodas and shrines built into the limestone Huong Tich mountains. It is sometimes known as 'The Mountain of the Fragrant Traces'. Many visitors find the journey

there, which involves bus, a romantic river-boat ride and a short hike, to be awe-inspiring.

It is the site of a very popular religious festival every March and April (from the middle of the second lunar month to the end of the third lunar month), drawing large numbers of pilgrims. Visiting the site itself feels very much like a pilgrimage. Hardy local women row little sampan boats with pairs of tourists for an hour up the river, which flows through beautiful limestone scenery. On the way, it is customary to stop at the 17th-century Trinh Temple complex, built in honour of the Trinh lords who helped fund the building work. A few minutes' walk away from the river along a stone path is the Chu Thien Chu, the 'Pagoda

A lacquered jackfruit-wood statue at the Tay Phuong Pagoda

Hanoi environs and excursions

Leading To Heaven'. It houses a superb stone statue of Quan Am, Goddess of Mercy, measuring almost 3m (10ft). The temple complex here has a calm, dignified feel to it, and provides quality time for the visitor to stroll around, taking in the fresh air away from the metropolis of Hanoi.

The hour's walk up to the Perfume Pagoda is lined with relatively expensive food and drink stalls, so remember to bring water for the 3km (2 mile) hike, as well as wearing sturdy shoes. Upon reaching the grotto, you gaze down from the top of 120 steps towards the massive cavern entrance. The dark recesses are filled with altars and statues of the Buddha.

60km (37 miles) southwest of Hanoi.

Follow Highway 6 through Ha Dong, then turn left on the QL21B heading south, to Duc Khe and the Suoi Yen boat station. Admission charge. Day-tours here often include lunch and entrance fees. Do not accept token gifts such as wrist bands from local women before you board the boat, as they will be waiting for you when you come back, expecting money!

Tam Coc

For those unable to visit Halong Bay (*see p68*), this is a fine alternative. Often described as 'Halong Bay without the water', it is a beautiful area with limestone peaks, caverns and river formations. As you glide along the river in a small sampan, it is hard to resist the romantic, serene atmosphere of the scenery.

The dramatic landscape in the Perfume Pagoda area

The film *Indochine* featured the stunning scenery of Tam Coc, and this has done wonders for the area's popularity. There is easy access to the area, with concreted canal banks as far as the first bridge, although something should be done about the overzealous embroidery-sellers who accompany you on your sampan. As you reach the end of the stretch of river after an hour and turn back, boats of drink-sellers will suggest that you buy a can for your thirsty sampan-rower. Make no doubt that the sampan-rower will return the can to the drink-seller as soon as the river ride ends. The river can also be toured on foot, with paths showing the way, and a number of temples and communal houses available to be visited.

Tam Coc means 'Three Caves', referring to the three long tunnel-caves that you pass along the journey (named Hang Ca, Hang Giua and Hang Cuoi). During the wet season, the tunnels are made even more claustrophobic by the swollen river, which barely gives boats room to clear the ceiling of the caves. *7km (4 miles) southwest of Ninh Binh, which is 95km (59 miles) south of Hanoi. A tour here often includes a visit to Hoa Lu, not far away.*

Hoa Lu

Hoa Lu was the capital of Vietnam under the Dinh Dynasty in the 10th century, then called Dai Co Viet. Although the fortified royal palaces are now in ruins there are still some splendid dynastic temples, built in remembrance of the

Ricefields near Tam Coc

kings, that are in good shape, having been restored in the 17th century to their 11th-century design.

The first of these, Den Dinh, devoted to the Emperor Dinh Tien Hoang, is an imposing building with a mysterious, well-decorated inner sanctuary. The emperor moved the capital of the country from Co Loa to the more secure location in this valley, away from Chinese attacks. In 979, he and his eldest sons were assassinated as they slept. The king was laid to rest in a royal sepulchre at the top of nearby Mount Ma Yen, which can be climbed, and offers stunning views over the valley.

The second temple, Den Le Dai Hanh, a short walk away, is dedicated to Le Dai Hanh, who seized power in the anarchy after Dinh Tien Hoang's assassination. He was commander of Dinh Tien Hoang's army and lover of his wife, declaring himself king in 980. *12km (7 miles) northwest of Ninh Binh. Open: 8am–5pm. Admission and parking charges.*

Northern Vietnam

Northern Vietnam has a wealth of stunning landscapes that should not be missed. Halong Bay is the most popular tourist attraction, with its spectacular limestone formations and mystical watery seascapes, but there is much else to see in the north. The hill tribes and scenery of the Far North offer experiences entirely new to most Westerners: colourful hill-tribe markets, learning about the lives of ethnic minorities and walking the unspoiled countryside around Sapa, Ba Be Lake and Dien Bien Phu, which are unrivalled in Vietnam.

HALONG BAY

A boat trip in Halong Bay is the highlight of many a visitor's trip to Vietnam. The beautiful scenery in its natural setting has attracted tourists from all over the world for hundreds of years. An overnight stay on a boat is well worth considering; the alternative is a very long day-trip, a large proportion of which will be spent sitting on a bus. In choosing a tour, remember that in general, you get what you pay for. Don't automatically choose the cheapest tour.

As a result of Halong Bay's popularity, changes are inevitably taking place. The journey from Hanoi, which used to take a whole day, now takes just three hours on the expressway. The bun-fight that characterises the landing dock in Halong city sees scores of tourist boats cramming together, ready for the boarding of hundreds of tourists taking virtually the same tour.

Fortunately, at 1,550sq km (598sq miles) the massive scale of Halong Bay makes it easy for boats to remain isolated from each other.

Background

Mythology has it that the bay was formed when the frolics of a dragon threw up this mishmash of rocky limestone peaks, totalling almost 2,000. The name Ha Long ('Dragon Descending') was coined as a result. For centuries visitors have eulogised the beauty of the bay; as early as 1469 King Le Thanh Tong wrote a poem about the bay after his visit.

The innumerable bays and coves within this rocky coastline were ideal bases for pirates for most of its history. It became a huge problem for the Vietnamese and Chinese rulers of the 18th century, whose armies failed to disperse the pirate armada of 50,000 men in hundreds of fighting boats. It was only with the arrival of the Royal Navy from Britain, sent from Hong Kong and Singapore to defend trading routes, that the pirates moved their activities inland.

The bay was declared a UNESCO World Heritage Site in 1994, and has been described as the eighth wonder of the world. With all this adulation, some people find their visit an anticlimax, especially when cloudy and rainy weather spoils the scenery. The weather can be unsettled during the winter from November, but the months to avoid particularly are February and March.

The topography of the bay is described technically as 'karst', created by the erosive effects of rainwater and underground rivers on the thick layer of shelly material formed by marine sedimentation. Ha Long is the largest marine karst in the world. The dominant vegetation in the area is saxifrage, a tough plant that survives the harsh terrain without the need for much soil.

Hang Thien Cung

Amongst the scores of caves in the area near Bai Chay this one, 'The Grotto of the Heavenly Place', is the most beautiful. Reached by a steep 50m (164ft) climb, it contains a rectangular chamber 250m (820ft) long, with delightfully coloured sections, and unusually shaped stalactite and stalagmite patterns. It was only discovered in 1993, and has been developed over the years using UNESCO funds to enable easier access.

Northern Vietnam

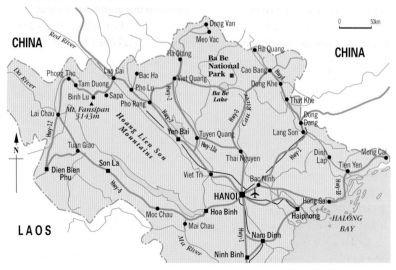

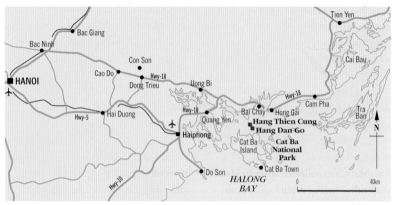

Hang Dan Go

On 'The Island of Marvels', the closest island to the mainland, is this famous grotto, the 'Grotto of the Wooden Stakes'. Before the crucial battle of Bach Dang River in 1288, in which he defeated the Mongols, General Tran Hung Dao amassed hundreds of sharpened poles, now displayed in the Haiphong Museum.

Cat Ba Island

Many tours spend a night on this, the largest island in Halong Bay. Given the choice, visitors would do better to stay the night on a boat or alternatively on one of the small island beaches that are used by some tours. The built-up nature of Cat Ba Town, with its concrete hotels, tends to spoil the atmosphere of what was originally a simple fishing port. However, there are attractions on the island, particularly its rugged, unspoilt coastal scenery. Also recommended are two pretty sandy beaches northeast of the port, uninspiringly called 'Cat Co I' and 'Cat Co II'. Popular with tours is the two- to three-hour hike from the headquarters of the Cat Ba National Park through the forest to Ech Lake. The most common trees in the forest are *kimgiao*, whose wood was famous for its use in the royal court in the past as chopsticks, because it reacts to poisons.

THE FAR NORTH

Today's travellers are not the first to visit this region. The issue of accessibility is something that troubled the French rulers when they first encountered this largely wild and mountainous area. However, the region has some of the most beautiful mountain scenery in Vietnam, and attractions such as the hill-tribe communities, the markets and the natural beauty of the area make a welcome change from Vietnam's city-bound attractions.

If you are on a tight schedule, the nearest you will come to visiting the far north may be a two-day tour of Sapa, easily the most accessible and visited part of the region. Lucky travellers who have more time to invest, however, will find their efforts to travel to areas such as Bac Ha, Dien Bien Phu and Ba Be Lake well rewarded.

Mai Chau

The Mai Chau valley is closer to Hanoi than other tourist destinations in the far north of the country, and so is a popular destination for visitors who do not have time to visit Sapa. Here, ethnic minority villages can be visited, and the unspoilt landscape – flat and filled with paddy fields, with mountains in the background – can be enjoyed.

Mai Chau was put on the tourist map in 1990, as one of the first market towns in the northwest to be accessible to tourists. Now, the locals are well versed in catering to the hordes of visitors who swamp the place, especially at weekends. The morning market is colourful and bustling, although the villagers do not wear their traditional dress any more.

The town of Mai Chau is not usually the base for tour groups, who tend to stay in the villages of Ban Lac or Pom Coong to the west of the town, particularly the former.

Ban Lac, a settlement of 70-odd houses, is home to the White Thai hill-tribe people, who produce attractive hand-woven textiles and put on a show of traditional dancing. The romantic feel of the village is balanced by the realisation that tourism rather than farming is what keeps the village prosperous. Staying there is enjoyable, with authentic stilt houses available as lodging, some specially adapted for Western home comforts. The thatched roofs and sounds of hens and other farm animals all add to the charm. Organised walking tours are available, or bicycle hire can be arranged to enable you to wander around the valley, visiting pretty villages such as Co Luong and Ban Van near Mai Chau town. *110km (68 miles) southwest of Hanoi, just off Highway 6. Buses take 4–5 hours.*

In and around Sapa

Sapa's growing popularity with tour-groups stems from its relatively

A woman weaving near the village of Mai Chau

Northern Vietnam

straightforward access via the railway between Hanoi and nearby Lao Cai, and the cool climate, which transformed the region into a French hill-station along the lines of Dalat. The attractions of the area are easy to identify: there are limitless opportunities for trekking among the beautiful scenery of remote valleys and isolated villages and hamlets, and for encountering fascinating hill-tribe peoples such as the Black H'mong and Red Dao.

The area is dominated geographically by Fansipan, at 3,143m (10,312ft) Vietnam's highest mountain, which rises up sharply from the Red River Valley. The French colonial elite used to have holiday homes in Sapa, but the hill-station disappeared during the war against China in 1979.

Sapa town

While the town is not the most quaint or attractive, it fulfils the practical purpose of being the base and lodging for treks into the surrounding area. It also possesses a large, covered permanent market that is popular with tourists. There are many Black H'mong, Red Dao and Giay hill-tribe people in town, but remember to ask permission before taking photos.

380km (236 miles) northwest of Hanoi. There are daytime and overnight sleeper trains every day to Lao Cai, taking 8–10 hours. Buses from Lao Cai train station make the hour's journey up the mountain to Sapa.

Treks

H'mong villages are numerous outside Sapa, and some are within walking

H'mong people in the market at Sapa

distance of town. One of the most popular is Cat Cat village, 3km (2 miles) walk away, directly below Sapa in the Muong Hoa Valley. Here, wooden houses nestle among bamboo and fruit trees. There is a waterfall just below, which is worth visiting.

To reach minorities other than the H'mong, you need to walk further afield. Ta Van Village is fascinating, as it contains both Giay and Dao communities. The 11km (7-mile) trek to this village down the Muong Hoa Valley is one of the most enjoyable in the area, with spectacular scenery and a wonderful climate. A wooden suspension bridge crosses the Muong Hoa River 2km (1¼ miles) before the village. Home-stays in this village are common and are a highlight of many visitors' trips.

Hoang Lien Son Nature Reserve

The reserve itself aims to protect the natural forest habitat of 30sq km (11½sq miles). Many of the 56 types of mammal in the reserve are rare or endangered species, and the reserve boasts some 150 bird species as well.

Mount Fansipan lies within the reserve boundaries, less than 5km (3 miles) from Sapa, but it is a tough three- to five-day climb. Those who brave the arduous trek through pine forest and bamboo thickets to climb the southern ridge are able to enjoy panoramas across the mountain ranges of northwest Vietnam and northwards towards Yunnan in China.

H'mong mother and daughter rest in the hills near Bac Ha

Bac Ha

This small town is well known for its lively Sunday market, when villagers from the Giay, Dao, Nung, Tay and Flower H'mong minorities descend on the town to buy and sell wares.

Many visitors choose to stay the whole weekend in the area to take in the colourful Saturday market at nearby Can Cau. The best time to visit the markets is between 10am and lunchtime.

Although the Bac Ha area is not as beautiful or high as that around Sapa, it is much less touristy and more authentic. The valley, with its cone-shaped mountains, is also attractive. *Bac Ha and Can Cau are 100km (62 miles) from Sapa, 40–45km (25–28 miles) northeast of Highway 7, past Pho Lu, in Lao Cai province.*

Northern ethnic minorities

Experiencing the simple rural life and traditional customs of the hill-tribe people in northern Vietnam is an eye-opener for many Westerners, and is often the favourite part of a tourist's visit. It is recommended that you visit one of the relevant museums in Hanoi for some initial education before the trip up north. They are the Museum of the Nationalities in Vietnam in Thai Nguyen (*open: Tue–Sun 8–11am and 2–4.30pm*), and the Museum of Ethnology, just outside Hanoi.

There are many ethnic groups in the mountainous regions of the north, all of them originating in southern China. Some of them, such as the Tay and Thai, farm the fertile valley bottom, while more isolated groups like the H'mong and Dao survive in the less hospitable higher altitudes. Almost 7 million people, making up two-thirds of Vietnam's minority population, live in the northern uplands.

The northwest

Dao (pronounced 'Zao'). This group numbers 600,000, and has some of the most striking traditional costumes. A rectangular patch of embroidery is sewn onto the back of jackets, and women wear elaborate headgear, embroidered or decorated with silver coins or tassels. Their unusual faces come from shaving their eyebrows and sometimes their whole head. They are a diverse people, living in small groups. They are instantly recognisable in the market at Sapa.

Giay (pronounced 'Zay'). This is a relatively small minority group of around 50,000, living in Lai Chau, Ha Giang and Lao Cai provinces in northwest Vietnam, often at high altitudes. Their society is feudal, and all villagers work on communal land. Traditional dress consists of bright green, pink or blue shirts, with a circular panel sewn around the collar.

H'mong These people are commonly found in the areas around Sapa, although they are scattered around many of the northern provinces. The meaning of their name, 'free people', originated from their fleeing from southern China at the end of the 18th century. They are some of the poorest of the minorities owing to their isolation from others and low-quality farmland. They are skilled hunters and gather products from the forest, as well as farming the land and raising livestock. They are best known for their silver jewellery and embroidered handicrafts. Men wear indigo clothing and women wear

A silver Vietnamese hill-tribe pendant

knee-length skirts, aprons and silver jewellery.

Muong The Muong live in the lower hills around Yen Bai, Son La towards Thanh Hoa, numbering about 1.2 million. Aristocratic families traditionally dominate the community, with drums and bronze gongs as symbols of their authority. They are famous for their embroidered fabrics with bold black-and-white geometric patterns. Older women wear traditional long black skirts.

Thai This group has 1.3 million people or so, living mostly in Son La and Lai Chau provinces, and distantly related to the Thai in Thailand. They have a long legacy of folklore and epic poems and are famous for their dance. Women learn how to weave and embroider from an early age, preparing blankets for their dowry. The Black Thai live around Son La and Dien Bien Phu while the White Thai are mainly based around Lai Chau and Mai Chau. Despite the names, these two groups in fact wear similar clothes, with long dark sarong-like skirts with a brightly coloured sash.

The northeast

Tay This is the country's largest highland minority group, with 1.6 million people, living mainly in the lowlands in the northeast. They are strongly influenced by Viet culture and few men wear traditional dress. The women wear the long, belted Tay dress of indigo-dyed cloth, with a plain headscarf and lots of silver jewellery. The Tay are well known for their fish-farming. Their irrigation systems include huge water wheels found beside rivers. Their customs include alternate singing (two choirs singing in alternation), kite-flying and traditional games.

Nung Closely related to the Tay, they share the same language and often live in the same villages. Their population is around 850,000 strong, living in Lang Son and Cao Bang provinces. They are reputed to be the best horticulturalists in the country, terracing the lower slopes to maximise harvests. They are also excellent blacksmiths. Their dress is similar to the Tay, with colourful neck scarves and bright shoulder bags.

Ba Be National Park

Ba Be National Park is one of the main natural attractions in the northeast of Vietnam, in an area which does not have the same pull on tourists as the northwest region around Sapa. This is partly due to the more difficult access, and partly because the landscape is not so dramatic. However, the rural landscapes are still lovely, with rugged limestone outcrops and ethnic minorities living off the pockets of cultivated land.

Ba Be Lake, at 7km (4 miles) long and 1km (²/₃ mile) wide, is Vietnam's largest natural lake, lying at the centre of the country's eighth national park. It is not on many tourist itineraries, owing to its long distance from Hanoi. This is a shame, because the park is full of outstanding natural beauty. Dense woods, white limestone cliffs and ancient trees, and a host of rare and endangered mammals, fish and plants, make this a wildlife lover's dream. Boat trips are easily arranged to visit nearby minority villages, waterfalls and caves. There are also little islands that can be visited, such as An Ma ('Horse's Saddle') Island.

Although one can reach the lake by road, a trip up the Song Nang River is recommended. The river threads through limestone cliffs, muddy hillocks overwhelmed by the jungle, and the twisted trunks of ancient trees, creepers and roots hanging over the water. You will pass the Tunnel Cave of Phuong, a 300m (984ft) bat-filled cave, formed by the river boring its way through the mountain. Beyond this is Dau Dang Waterfall, a beautiful but dangerous section of rapids. The nearby Tay village is ideal for an overnight stay in a stilt house.

Ba Be Lake is about 160km (99 miles) north of Hanoi, a 6-hour drive. Some tours include the lake within a four- to five-day tour of Cao Bang and Lang Son provinces. Public transport to the area is limited.

Dien Bien Phu and around

Close to the Lao border is the historic battlefield of Dien Bien Phu, one of the few sights in the far north of Vietnam. However, the surrounding scenery is every bit as interesting, with sweeping valleys and grand mountains. Not

THE BATTLE OF DIEN BIEN PHU

This crucial battle in May 1954 ended the French occupation of Vietnam, and gave the Vietnamese an important bargaining tool at the Geneva Convention in the same month. The French, under General Navarre, hoped to draw the Viet Minh out into the open by basing French parachute battalions in heavily fortified positions in the middle of the valley at Dien Bien Phu. Meanwhile, the Viet Minh under General Giap quietly transported heavy artillery and troops across mountains and jungle, to the slopes overlooking the base. The Viet Minh pounded the French positions, and, fighting doggedly for every inch of ground, slowly wore down the French into submission. After 59 days of siege, Navarre's garrison surrendered, and ten months later the French left Vietnam, signalling the end of their colonial rule of Indochina altogether.

many make the two-day bus journey from Hanoi to this remote region, although some tourists, mostly French visitors interested in the wartime sites, take the short flight from Hanoi.

Dien Bien Phu sits in a heart-shaped valley measuring 19km (12 miles) by 8km (5 miles). The town itself is growing rapidly, not because of tourism, but because of the lucrative smuggling that takes place over the border with Laos, only 35km (22 miles) away.

There are several sights in and around the town relating to the famous battle in 1954. The town's museum shows some fascinating wartime photos of the valley, as well as weaponry and equipment from the time, including a bicycle adapted to carry huge loads of supplies to Viet Minh troops.

Opposite the museum is the Viet Minh Cemetery with simple grey marble headstones.

A small hill overlooking the cemetery is also worth a visit. Called 'Hill A1' by the Vietnamese and 'Eliane 2' by the French, it was the scene of bitter hand-to-hand fighting and was eventually overrun by the Viet Minh. A tank from the battle is on display, as well as a reconstructed bunker and various memorials. The panorama over the fertile valley below is lovely.

Many visitors to Dien Bien Phu also travel 100km (62 miles) east to Son La, a charming town on the edge of a valley. It contains an old French prison, as well as nearby caves and minority villages that are worth visiting.

Entrance to the Viet Minh war cemetery, Dien Bien Phu

Hué

Hué has much to offer. The Imperial City was once a magnificent centre of the royal court, situated in the heart of a walled citadel, protected on all sides by moats. Hué's time as capital of Vietnam and home to its emperors meant that a series of superb royal mausoleums was built outside the city, along the banks of the Perfume River. Hué's cuisine is famed throughout the land, and its status as a UNESCO World Heritage Site means that visitors will find restaurants and hotels of a high standard.

Many visitors only spend a couple of days in this charming city, often stopping off midway in Vietnam as part of their journey between Hanoi and Ho Chi Minh City. A few visitors are put off by the very wet climate that the area suffers from, especially between October and December, and also from relatively high entrance fees to its sights. As well as having many sights of its own, Hué is also a transport hub and an excellent base for visiting places in the surrounding area, such as the Demilitarised Zone (DMZ) and Hoi An.

The city is divided into three main sections. The Citadel sits on the northwestern bank of the Perfume River and contains the historic Imperial City at its southeastern end, the focus of much of the sightseeing in the city. Across the Perfume River is what was called the European city, which is the commercial heart of Hué, containing the bulk of the city's hotels, restaurants, tour offices and internet cafés. Lastly, to the east of the Citadel, is Phu Cat, the original merchants' quarter of Hué.

History

The area around Hué belonged to the Champa kingdom until 1306, but from

HUÉ CUISINE

There are three distinct types of Hué cuisine: 'Imperial meals', the dishes originating from the emperor's court, 'frugal meals' (as they are called) available from local stalls and street kitchens, and vegetarian food prepared in the pagodas.

According to legend, one of the emperors insisted that all his meals consist of 50 different dishes prepared by 50 different chefs. Imperial meals are available from some of the large upmarket hotels such as the historic Saigon Morin (*see p82*) – at a price. Hué's most famous dish is *banh khoai*, a yellow pancake with shrimp, pork and beansprouts, served with lettuce, mint leaves and a peanut and sesame sauce – as delicious as it sounds. Also recommended are special snacks, such as *banh nam*, made with rice-flour dough topped with spices and morsels of shrimp and pork, steamed in a banana leaf.

1558 the town was ruled by the Nguyen lords, who dominated Southern Vietnam for 200 years. By the late 17th century Phu Xuan, as the town was then called, was a major cultural centre. Hué's position really took off when Emperor Gia Long, who founded the Nguyen dynasty, moved the capital of Vietnam here in an attempt to unify the country. It was in these golden years that extravagant royal buildings were built, and the city became known not only for its luxurious palaces but also as a seat of learning.

Hué became a focal point for opposition to French rule, and also for resistance to the American-backed presidency of Diem in the 1960s, which was brutally suppressed. In 1963 government troops fired into crowds of protestors, and many of the Buddhist clergy were arrested and imprisoned. The city's tragic modern history continued during the American War, when it was captured by Northern Vietnamese troops during the 1968 Tet Offensive and occupied for a month. Hué was retaken in perhaps the most bitter battle of the whole war, which left up to 10,000 people dead, both civilian and military, and the historic citadel almost flattened.

Hué

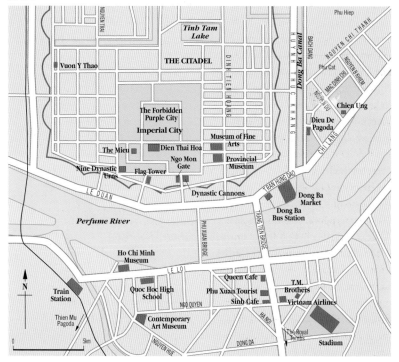

The Ngo Mon Gate, southern entrance to the Imperial Enclosure

Hué's rich heritage is slowly being rebuilt with UNESCO aid and it is now justifiably a premier tourist destination.

THE IMPERIAL CITY

Within the citadel lie a second moat and defensive wall that enclose the Imperial City, with a symmetrical layout that copies Beijing's Forbidden City. It was known as Dai Noi, 'the Great Enclosure', and was home to the emperor and his court of mandarins, servants and advisers. The passage of time, especially during the American War, which devastated the town, has not treated this once magnificent complex kindly. Out of 148 buildings in the complex, only 20 were left standing at the end of the war. Those that have been restored look magnificent again, while others only hint at the grandeur of the past. Other areas are overgrown with grass, with only remnants of foundations and ruined walls.

Southern Gate (Ngo Mon)

Out of the four gates in the Great Enclosure, the most impressive is this, the south-facing Ngo Mon, the main and highly dramatic entrance to the Imperial City. It was built in 1833 by Emperor Minh Mang and heavily restored in 1990. The gate itself has five entrances, the central one for the emperor alone, a couple of massive openings for the royal elephants, and another pair for the mandarins.

On top of the pavilion is the 'Five Phoenix Watchtower', with nine roofs said to resemble five birds in flight. It was in this pavilion that the last Nguyen emperor, Bao Dai, abdicated in 1945. The colours of the porcelain roof tiles refer to the king (yellow) and mandarins (green).

Palace of Supreme Harmony (Dien Thai Hoa)

This spectacular palace was highly important in its day, as it was the throne palace where major ceremonies took place. The emperor would sit on a raised dais under a gilded canopy, facing south across the 'Esplanade of Great Salutations', a courtyard where mandarins would stand, civil on the left and military on the right.

First constructed in 1805, rescue work took place in 1991 to replace the 80 wooden pillars in the throne room, which had been damaged by termites. The pillars are lacquered in red and gold, with poems in Chinese script decorating them. In the back room is a fascinating scale model showing what the Imperial City would have looked like at its pinnacle.

Dynastic Temple (The Mieu)

This low building, erected in 1822, was given over to the worship of the Nguyen emperors during Minh Mang's reign. Each of the ten wooden altars is devoted to a different emperor, with some including a portrait or photo of the monarch. Anniversaries of the deaths of the emperors are still commemorated here.

The Nine Dynastic Urns

These gigantic 3ft (1m) urns are located in the southwest corner of the Imperial City and are considered to be the finest example of Hué's craftsmanship. Cast in bronze during the reign of Minh Mang, each is dedicated to an emperor and each has slightly different feet and handles. The heaviest, at 2,600kg (5,732lbs), honours Emperor Gia Long.

The Forbidden Purple City

Only a handful of buildings remains of this once stunning 40-building complex

in the heart of the Imperial City. It would have been reserved for the royal family, with no one else being allowed to enter other than mandarin-eunuchs. The area would have contained residential palaces, with living quarters for the state physician and nine ranks of royal concubines.

Immediately behind the Palace of Supreme Harmony are two buildings facing each other across a courtyard. Here, mandarins would prepare themselves before seeing the emperor. The 'Right House' contains ornate murals, some fascinating old photos of Hué, and a display of magnificent imperial silk robes. Just northeast is the 'Thai Binh Reading Pavilion', a two-tier structure surrounded by bonsai gardens, built by Emperor Thieu Tri.

One of the Nine Dynastic Urns

Walk: The Imperial City

This walk takes you from the 'European city', east of the Perfume River, where the majority of hotels are situated, into the Citadel. The highlights of the Imperial City are covered, eventually taking you out by the east gate. This walk is ideal in the morning, finishing just in time for lunch.

Allow 3 hours.

Start on the east bank of the Perfume River, in front of the Saigon Morin Hotel.

1 Saigon Morin Hotel

This historic hotel is now over 100 years old, a superb example of French colonial architecture. The interior is worth visiting if you have time, if only to admire the chic ambience.

Walk over Trang Tien Bridge to the west bank of the Perfume River, turning left onto Tran Hung Dao. You will soon see the grand Southern Gate on your right.

2 The Dynastic Cannons

Through the Ngan Gate is a grand parade-ground, with nine dynastic cannons, superbly crafted in bronze. You will see the highly symbolic Flag Tower on your left. It was here that the Viet Cong briefly flew the Communist flag during the American War.

Turn left onto 23 Thang 8 towards the Southern Gate.

3 Southern Gate (Ngo Mon)

This is the most impressive of the ten gates around the citadel. Just imagine the occasion when the emperor walked through his

Map labels:

Dien Tho
Hang Mieu
Right House
Thai Binh Reading Pavilion
Royal Theater
DOAN THI DIEM
Left House
Dien Thai Hoa
Hien Nhon Gate
DINH CONG TRANG
The Mieu
Hien Lam Cac
Ngo Mon Gate
Museum of Fine Arts
DINH TIEN HOANG
ONG ICH KHIEM
Ngan Gate
LE TRUC
Dynastic Cannons
LE DUAN
TRAN HUNG DAO
N
PHU XUAN BRIDGE
TRANG TIEN BRIDGE
LE LOI
Saigon Morin Hotel

personal gateway, with royal elephants lumbering under the massive gates at either end. You can climb the steep steps to the Five Phoenix Watchtower to admire the view.

Walk over the Trung Dao bridge that spans Thai Dich Lake, into the stone courtyard, the Esplanade of Great Greetings.

4 Palace of Supreme Harmony (Dien Thai Hoa)

In front of this ceremonial square is the magnificent Thai Hoa Palace, a sumptuously decorated ceremonial hall. *Behind this palace is a courtyard where the Great Golden Gate would have stood. Walk along the avenue to the right.*

5 Dynastic Temple (The Mieu)

Next door to the Hung Temple is this lovely temple dedicated to the worship of the Nguyen emperors. Also worth seeing are the Nine Dynastic Urns, in front of the Pavilion of Splendour opposite (*see p81*).

With your back to the Chuong Duc Gate, walk northeast along the path for 50m (55yds) or so, looking left.

6 The Forbidden Purple City

Within the Forbidden Purple City, one of the most interesting buildings is the 'Right House', named because out of the two facing buildings used by mandarins, this was on the emperor's right from his viewpoint.

Continuing east, walk 200m (220 yds) or so out of the Imperial City through the East Gate. Look for the superb palace immediately on your right.

7 Museum of Fine Arts

This museum is worth a quick visit, to look at the array of artefacts from the imperial court.

From here you turn right at the next block, onto D Dinh Tien Hoang, which takes you to the river, passing several cheap restaurants that are known for their delicious food and friendly atmosphere. Just the spot for lunch.

The Palace of Supreme Harmony, Imperial City

THE CITADEL

Consisting of 520 hectares (1,285 acres) enclosed within a 7m (23ft) high, 20m (66ft) thick wall, the citadel is surrounded by a moat and canal. Construction began in 1805 with the help of French engineers, and thousands of workers were used over the next 30 years to construct more than 300 buildings, many of them situated within the Imperial City.

Now the citadel is a pleasant area to walk and cycle around, being relatively free of traffic. There are pretty lakes and gardens, as well as the occasional shop and hotel. Not many people choose to stay within the citadel walls, but it is a tranquil area and an ideal base for visiting the sights in the Imperial City.

The Flag Tower (Cot Co)

This is the citadel's most prominent feature and dominates the southern battlements. It is not a flag tower as such, but three squat brick terraces with a 17.5m (57ft) flagpole. It was here that the Viet Cong flag briefly flew during the 1968 Tet Offensive during the American War.

The Dynastic Cannons

Just east of the Flag Tower is the Ngan Gate, through which is a parade ground flanked by nine cannons. These were cast by Emperor Gia Long from bronze weapons taken from the Tay Son army following the rebellion of the same name in the 18th century. They were never meant to be fired, but rather venerated, each being given the title of 'Champion All-Powerful General'. They symbolise the four seasons and five ritual elements (earth, fire, metal, wood and water).

On the other side of the Flag Tower to the west is the Sap Gate where there is another set of cannons.

Museum of Fine Arts

This excellent museum is housed in the beautiful Long An Palace, originally built in 1845 and renovated in 1995. It contains around 500 artefacts from the period of the Nguyen dynasty, including household pottery and crockery, porcelain vases, furniture and embroidered clothes.
3 Le Truc. Open: daily 7am–6pm. Admission charge.

Provincial Museum

The exhibits here, in what was formerly the Military Museum, illustrate

Hue's famous Flag Tower in the Citadel

important chapters in Hué's history. Of particular interest are memorabilia from the demonstrations in 1963, which led to a crackdown on Buddhist dissenters, and from the 1968 battle for the city during the American War. Original film footage and photos all give added resonance to the tragic events that Hué has witnessed during the last 50 years.

23 Thang 8. Open: daily 7.30am–5.00pm. Admission charge.

Tinh Gia Vien Restaurant

Although not strictly a tourist sight, this magnificent restaurant deserves a mention not only because of its superb setting in a French colonial mansion, but also because it famously specialises in traditional dishes from Hué's imperial court. The artistic presentation of the food will leave you undecided whether to eat it or photograph it. Set dinners served by waitresses in traditional costume are pricy but a dining experience worth savouring.

20/3 D Le Thanh Ton. A 10-minute walk, just east of Imperial City.

THE ROYAL TOMBS

A visit to at least a couple of the royal tombs outside Hué should not be missed. It gives you a chance to get out of the city into the verdant countryside, and also to appreciate the importance that these mausoleums held for the Nguyen dynasties.

There are many organised day-trips to the tombs, not only by boat and bus but also motorbike tours. If the weather isn't too wet, you can hire your own motorbike or bicycle and find your own way around the bumpy roads and paths. Most of the tombs are south of Hué, dotted around the hills east of the Perfume River.

It is fair to say that the Nguyen emperors were preoccupied with the afterlife, and gave considerable thought to planning and building of their mausoleums. In fact, some emperors used them as secondary residences during their lives.

All the tombs were modelled on those of Chinese sovereigns, with a common blueprint, despite having variations that reflected the personality and tastes of each emperor. Each tomb complex had an outer wall, with a large 'Courtyard of Honour' with statues of mandarins lined up around it. At the end of the courtyard is usually a stele (inscribed stone slab) inside a tower, with engravings describing the achievements of the deceased king. There would also be a temple to honour the monarch, his queens and concubines, which housed the funerary tablets and altar. A low walled enclosure would usually house the emperor's tomb.

Tu Duc's Tomb

This tomb is in one of the most attractive settings, with a 12-hectare (30-acre) park containing serene lakes, pine forests and roughly 50 buildings. He spent 16 years enjoying the solitude, writing poetry, meditating and fishing.

Apparently he also found time to write philosophy and history, and enjoy 50-course meals and 104 wives, plus many more concubines. Needless to say, he wasn't a particularly effective monarch. He drove his 6,000 workers so hard in the construction of the mausoleum complex that they rebelled against him in 1866.

Xung Khiem Pavilion stands on the banks of the pretty Luu Khiem Lake. (Khiem means 'modest', a word used in all the names of the buildings in this complex.) Hoa Khiem Palace was used by the royal family and now contains some personal belongings of the king. There is a classical theatre within Minh Khiem Pavilion, which used to stage performances for the emperor and his courtiers; the stage and balcony can still be seen.

To the north is a second group of buildings with a salutation court, stele-house and then the emperor's tomb itself. Emperor Tu Duc was unusual in that he wrote his own eulogy, a lengthy piece of writing describing the many challenges throughout his reign.

Stairs leading to Emperor Khai Dinh's tomb

7km (4 miles) south of Hué by road, on the west bank of the Perfume River. Open: daily 7am–6pm. Admission charge. If coming by boat, you will need to walk 20 mins from the river bank or take a xe om *from there.*

Khai Dinh's Tomb

This mausoleum is in stark contrast, due to its lack of harmony. It attempts to blend traditional Vietnamese style with Western touches, resulting in a gaudy mishmash that sticks out in the surrounding landscape.

It is therefore not surprising to learn that Emperor Khai Dinh was a vain man, a puppet of the French colonials, who had to levy additional taxes from his people in order to pay for his mausoleum. While he only reigned for 9 years, the mausoleum took 11 years to complete, being finished in 1931.

The complex only has one main structure, the principal temple, a dark exterior which belies the extravagant interior, full of porcelain and glass mosaics. A lavish life-size bronze statue of the emperor dominates the main room.

10km (6 miles) south of Hué by road. Open: daily 7am–6pm. Admission charge.

Minh Mang's Tomb

The personality of the emperor is reflected in this mausoleum complex, one of the most attractive of the royal tombs. Minh Mang was the second Nguyen Emperor, passionate about architecture, painting and philosophy, serious and authoritarian, distrustful of the West. He designed his mausoleum along traditional Chinese lines, with the grandeur of the red-roofed buildings balanced by the lovely 15 hectares (37 acres) of landscaped gardens. Although he planned the mausoleum himself, construction only began after his death in 1841. He fathered 142 children with his 33 wives and 107 concubines.

There are 35 buildings, bridges, canals and ponds in this complex, laid out along a 700m (2,297ft) long axis. This processional route first visits the principal temple, then the 'Pavilion of Pure Light' (Minh Lau), and beyond this two stone gardens, a lake and the ceremonial burial ground.

12km (7 miles) south of Hué. Open: daily 7am–6pm. Admission charge.

Thien Mu Pagoda

OTHER SIGHTS OUTSIDE HUÉ
Thien Mu Pagoda

This pagoda is famous for a variety of reasons. It is the oldest pagoda in Hué, founded in 1601 by Nguyen Hoang. It has a peaceful setting by the river, with great views afforded by the terrace, while the large red-brick octagonal tower is clearly seen from miles around. Each of its seven storeys represents one of Buddha's reincarnations. It was built in 1840.

Nearby are two smaller towers, one of which houses a 2.5m (8ft) bell weighing over 2 tonnes, cast in 1710, which is audible from the city.

In the 1930s and '40s the pagoda was the centre of opposition to the French colonials from the Buddhists, who championed the people's grievances. This came to a dramatic head when in 1963 monk Thich Quang Duc drove from the temple to Saigon in his Austin car and burned himself to death at a busy junction, an act that shocked the world. This was the beginning of the end for President Diem. The blue Austin car is on display, together with a copy of the famous photograph from that fateful day.

6km (4 miles) southwest of Hué. Open: daily 7am–6pm. Admission charge. Most visitors come by boat, although it is near enough to the city to cycle here.

Central Provinces

Many visitors to Vietnam with limited time on their hands take the Reunification Express train from Hanoi to Hué, or fly between the two, and then perhaps take another flight from Hué to Ho Chi Minh City. By doing so they miss out a large number of important sights within the Central Provinces. These include the charming town of Hoi An, the Phong Nha cave system, the so-called DMZ, Bach Ma National Park and the Cham Towers at My Son.

The most important of these is Hoi An, a veritable living museum and increasingly popular with travellers for its laid-back atmosphere and great-value tailors.

Also not included in the typical two- to three-week itinerary of most travellers is the Demilitarised Zone or DMZ area, a particularly important site for those interested in the American War. Phong Nha Cave is a UNESCO World Heritage Site, while the mystical Cham Towers at My Son are a popular day-trip from Hoi An. For nature lovers, Bach Ma National Park is ideal for walking and ecotourism. You should try to include at least a couple of these sights, as they take you off the main tourist trail and give you the chance to travel in the 'real' Vietnam. The bus journey between Hué and Hoi An is also recommended, as it passes through

Part of the Phong Nha cave complex

stunning scenery on a clear day at Hai Van Pass, with opportunities to stop at China Beach and Marble Mountain.

PHONG NHA CAVE

The cave system in this area, only fully explored in 1992, has been added to the list of UNESCO World Heritage sites, which has helped attract more visitors in recent years. For those travelling independently and not on an organised tour, getting here is not easy. There are no sleeper trains from Hanoi to Dong Hoi, the nearest town, which leaves you the option of taking the overnight bus from Hanoi and arriving at Dong Hoi in the early hours of the morning, or taking an uncomfortable slow train. It is

possible that more convenient transport options will be made available as the sight's popularity increases.

The caves held a fascination for the local people from as early as the 9th century, in the days of the Cham empire, when they were thought to hold guardian spirits. During the American War they were used as a place of refuge from the bombing, as evidenced by rocket damage by the main cave entrance.

Phong Nha Cave, which has given its name to the whole cave system here, is the biggest and most beautiful. Many visitors take a boat from the landing stage 5km (3 miles) from the cave for a peaceful 30-minute ride that ends

Central Provinces

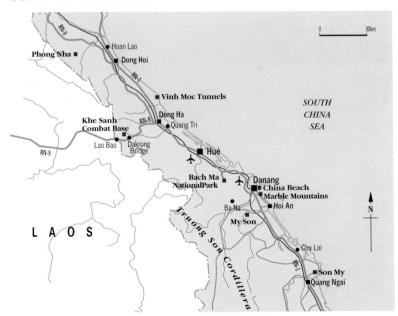

600m (1,969ft) within the cave. The sheer scale of the cave is awe-inspiring, and clever use of coloured spotlights illustrates the beauty of the limestone walls, with immense stalactites and stalagmites. The cave contains sandy beaches and grottoes, as well as a dry section for a short walk back to the entrance.

Dong Hoi is 488km (303 miles) south of Hanoi, and 166km (103 miles) north of Hué. The caves are less than 50km (31 miles) west of Dong Hoi.

THE DMZ

The Demilitarised Zone (DMZ) was a strip of no-man's land created in 1954, dividing the Communist North of Vietnam from the non-Communist South. The Geneva Accords, signed by the French and the Vietnamese in 1954, drew a provisional demarcation line along the 17th Parallel. This effectively ran along the Ben Hai River, with 5km (3 miles) either side of the line being the DMZ. In fact, the DMZ was anything but demilitarised after 1965 – the region was the scene of the most bitter fighting and the heaviest bombing during the American War.

Today, the area is becoming increasingly popular, especially for tour groups wishing to see some of the war sites, museums and memorials dotted around the area. Chief among these are the Vinh Moc Tunnels and the Khe Sanh battle site. Also in the same region are the remnants of the Ho Chi Minh

The DMZ

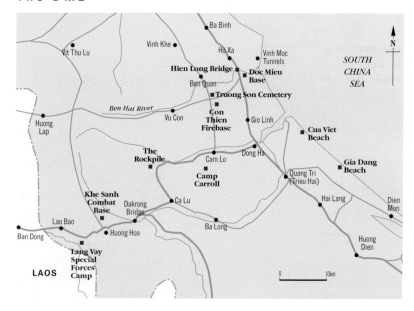

Trail and former US bases such as The Rockpile and Con Thien Firebase.

During the war, the DMZ was of huge strategic importance to both sides. The North sent huge numbers of troops and amounts of supplies over the border to South Vietnam via the Ho Chi Minh Trail, while the US tried desperately to stop this movement by breaking up supply routes and bombing Communist bases in the North. Massive bombing of the area by artillery and aircraft, directed by 'firebases' on strategic hills, did little to stop the flow of Communist supplies. In addition, thousands of tonnes of napalm and herbicide were dropped in an attempt to rob the Viet Cong (the North Vietnamese army) of the cover of jungle and forest. For many years afterwards, little was able to grow in the poisoned soil of the area. The impact of the war on the area is not only ecological. Since 1975, up to 20,000 local people have been killed by unexploded ordnance and mines in the DMZ, and the birth of deformed babies has also been a tragic problem.

The main sights of the DMZ can be visited on a day's tour, which is most commonly booked from Hué. Although Dong Ha is the nearest town to the DMZ, it is a sprawling, ugly place and sensibly avoided by most visitors to the area. Tours are the best way to explore the area, and indeed a local guide is recommended at the very least. Visitors should not walk around unguided, as some sites are not marked, and there is still the risk of unexploded ordnance.

Vinh Moc Tunnels

This is perhaps the most popular site in the DMZ, an amazing complex of tunnels used during the American War to provide shelter, mainly for civilians in surrounding villages, from the massive US bombing of the area. Two kilometres (1 1/4 miles) of tunnels were built from 1967 onwards, housing over 1,000 people for weeks on end. A section of the tunnels has been restored and can be visited. Those of a sensitive or claustrophobic disposition will be reassured that the tunnels are relatively well lit, well signposted and much bigger than the Cu Chi tunnels outside of Ho Chi Minh City. In fact, the tour only takes 15 minutes, exiting on the shores of the beach.

There is a small museum with photographs and memorabilia, illustrating the amazing tenacity and resourcefulness of the villagers during the war. All 650 inhabitants of nearby Vinh Moc village sheltered here, with several babies being born underground. There are three levels to the tunnel system, the first housing soldiers, the second villagers and the third, and deepest, used as stores for supplies and weapons. Each family was allocated a tiny cavern the size of a single bed. The underground village, however, still housed amenities such as a school, meeting rooms, a hospital and freshwater wells.

Central Provinces

Ho Xa township, 7km (4 miles) north of Ben Hai River and 28km (17 miles) from Dong Ha. Coming from the south, a signpost indicates a right-hand turn, leading to the tunnels after 15km (9 miles). Museum open: daily 7am–5pm. Admission charge.

Hien Long Bridge

The Ben Hai River that marked the 17th Parallel was crossed by this bridge, a highly symbolic landmark during the war. At the time, the bridge was both a physical and an ideological barrier separating the two Vietnams. Half the bridge was painted red, half yellow. On the southern banks is a memorial to those killed when the police station on the site was bombed, sited in the actual bomb crater. The current iron girder bridge is a reconstruction dating from 1973, the original having been destroyed in 1967.
Highway 1, 20km (12 miles) north of Dong Ha.

Khe Sanh Combat Base

The windswept plateau just south of the DMZ is overlooked by forested mountains that peak at Khe Sanh. Now just a bleak settlement, it was the setting of one of the key battles in the American War. On the site of the battle is a museum and memorial park, in which sit US wartime helicopters, artillery pieces and a reconstructed bunker.

Khe Sanh was used by the US Army as a forward base near Laos, to break

War relics at the Khe Sanh museum

up the Ho Chi Minh Trail supply route and call in bombardments onto the surrounding plateau. A massive build-up of NVA troops in 1967 threw the American leadership into a panic. They feared that if they lost the ensuing battle, it would be compared to the crucial French colonial defeat at Dien Bien Phu. President Johnson famously swore that he didn't want 'any damn Dinbinfoo'. The US threw huge numbers of troops and bombers into the fray, crucially diverting forces from the defence of other southern towns. Although the NVA sustained huge losses and abandoned their siege after 70 days, they took advantage of the resulting weakness of the southern towns during the Tet Offensive soon after. The Americans, meanwhile, withdrew from Khe Sanh three months after the battle, bulldozing the base flat and leaving a desolate landscape.

The battle's importance was twofold. It was seen as a test of US military credibility, which on the surface the US maintained, but it also demonstrated to the American generals – and most importantly to the Western media – that they could not win the war. *Museum 24km (15 miles) north of Khe Sanh town, which is on Highway 9, 63km (39 miles) west of Dong Ha. Open: daily 7am–5pm. Admission charge.*

Quang Tri (Trieu Hai)

Another war site, although not on many DMZ tours, is the town of Quang Tri, now known as Trieu Hai. The area was the scene of heavy fighting, not only during the American War, but also during the French War in the 1950s. The French dubbed the stretch of Highway 1 north of Hué *la rue sans joie* (street without joy), after suffering heavy losses from Viet Minh guerrilla

forces along the coast. In 1972 Communist forces captured the town of Quang Tri from the ARVN (South Vietnamese army) during their Easter Offensive. American B52 bombers pounded the town, reducing it to rubble in four months, with massive loss of life, both military and civilian.

The sights in Quang Tri include the Citadel, originally built in 1806, the remains of the 19th-century prison, and a small war museum. There are some very good photos from the war here, although there are no captions in English. East of the road is the small shell of Long Hung Church, a memorial to the victims of the battle. A track on the opposite side of the

Continued on p96

Rusting tanks near the old DMZ

The Ho Chi Minh Trail

The Ho Chi Minh Trail was conceived in early 1959 as a safe route by which to direct men and equipment down the length of Vietnam in support of Communist groups in the south. It was a vital supply route that enabled the Northern Vietnamese to win the war.

The Trail was in fact a complex network of many trails, mostly through jungle, which were successively widened throughout the war to increase the amount of supplies going through. At first, bicycles carrying huge loads were used, then night-time convoys of lorries as the quality of the tracks improved. As well as supplies, large numbers of Northern Vietnamese used the Trail to infiltrate the South – by 1967 100,000 a year were entering the South in this way. This infiltration was such that by 1970 it was said that if the Southern

Old US bomb casings littering the Trail have been adapted to many peaceful uses, such as fencing and as plant pots (right)

government were switched to a Communist one, there would not be much of a change in faces.

The length of the Trail has been estimated at 15,000km (9,320 miles), with hospitals, warehouses and petrol dumps dotted along the route. There was even a 200km (124-mile) long fuel pipeline. For much of its southerly route the trail ran through Laos and Cambodia, always through the most difficult, mountainous terrain. Unfortunately, these two countries were dragged into the war and

A model of a North Vietnamese soldier on the Ho Chi Minh Trail

received the most intense bombing. Aerial bombardment of the Trail by the US had begun in 1965, using napalm and defoliants as well as conventional bombs. In eight years the US Air Force dropped over two million tonnes of bombs, mostly over Laos, in an effort to cut the flow. Although the NVA suffered high casualties, the Trail was never completely severed. As soon as the bombing finished, trails were re-routed or repaired, and troop and supply movements continued.

highway leads 4km (2 1/2 miles) south to the ruins of La Vang Church, with a strange monument consisting of mushrooms, apparently representing the Virgin Mary's apparition to persecuted Catholics here in 1798. *Quang Tri town, 60km (37 miles) north of Hué. Long Hung Church is 5km (3 miles) south of the town. The Citadel and museum are open daily with admission charge.*

Truong Son Cemetery

A cemetery on this site is dedicated to the estimated 25,000 people who died on the Ho Chi Minh Trail, known by the Vietnamese as the Truong Son Trail. The 14-hectare (35-acre) cemetery is divided into five geographical regions and then by native province. Each headstone is marked with details of each *liet si* or martyr. On the way to the cemetery, you will pass Con Thien Firebase, the scene of yet another grim battle in which heavy shelling and carpet-bombing were used to defend positions from the NVA.
35km (22 miles) northwest of Dong Ha. Drive west along Highway 9, then turn north at Cam Lo on Highway 15 for 22km (14 miles).

BETWEEN HUÉ AND HOI AN
Bach Ma National Park

This eco-tourist destination contains a huge number of species of flora and fauna, which received formal protection when a national park was created in 1991. It is, however, an incredibly wet area, with a high level of rainfall and some chilly temperatures, especially at the higher levels of the park. The Asiatic Black Bear is one of the 83 mammal, 230 bird and 1,400 flora species that make their home here in 22,000 hectares (54,363 acres) of lush forest.

The area was popular with the French colonials, who set up a mountain resort in 1936. Emperor Bao Dai also kept some luxury villas in the area. It fell into disrepair during the war years, but the area is being redeveloped for the tourist trade. The well-organised series of trails makes it ideal for walking and bird-watching right up the mountain to the summit, where there are breathtaking views of the whole area.

The Marble Mountains and China Beach

This is a regular stop for buses taking visitors between Hué and Hoi An. The most southerly limestone outcrops in the country are located here. The walk up to the caves takes 20–30 minutes; the views from the top are great, although the caves themselves are not awe-inspiring. The Cham people came here regularly for pilgrimage, as did the Nguyen kings. Marble from the mountain was used in the construction of Ho Chi Minh's mausoleum. The highest mountain is Thuy Son, with a pagoda in the middle of a series of grottoes at the top. The most impressive of the cave pagodas is Huyen Khong Cave.

Just a few kilometres north of Marble Mountains lies China Beach, also known as My Khe beach. It is the nearest beach resort to Danang, Vietnam's main port and its third-largest city. There is little to see in Danang, and most travellers merely pass through it on a bus or taxi to Danang airport, just outside the city centre, for internal flights around the country. China Beach is often shrouded in mist and cannot be seen from the road, but on a clear day the views down to the beach are superb. China Beach was well known to American servicemen during the war as an 'R & R' base.

The Marble Mountains are 12km (7 miles) southeast of Danang. China Beach is 3km (2 miles) southeast of Danang.

HOI AN

This charming town on the banks of the Thu Bon River is growing ever more popular with tourists, having been named a UNESCO World Heritage Site in 1999. Its attractions include a rich architectural heritage from its days as a bustling 16th-century trading port, a quaint atmosphere that seems magically to step back in time, a beach at nearby Cua Dai, and Champa ruins just a bus ride away at My Son.

Hoi An is also ideally placed near the tourist centre of Hué, which is just a few hours on the road north. A nearby domestic airport at Danang, less than an hour's drive away, makes Hoi An easily accessible to most tourists on a whistle-stop tour of Vietnam and a good base for a visit to the area.

As a result of its popularity, hotels are springing up all over Hoi An, female shopkeepers cheerily try to

HOI AN'S TICKET SCHEME

This scheme contributes to the preservation of the old centre. A single ticket allows access to five sights in the town, out of a choice of 12 participating sights. You can visit one of the merchant houses, one museum, a handicrafts workshop, one of the Chinese Assembly Halls, and either the Japanese Covered Bridge or the Chua Ong. Tickets are on sale at six outlets dotted around the old town.

View of China Beach from the Marble Mountains

persuade you to look at their tailor's shop or art gallery and the streets are awash with tourists clasping ever-expanding bags of bargain souvenirs and clothes. Shopaholics should be warned that they are likely to spend longer than they planned in this charming town. The abundance of incredibly cheap tailors, who will run up whatever you want overnight, and the huge range of shops and restaurants in quaint streets, are likely to keep you in the town for at least a couple of days.

Hoi An's fortunes have waxed and waned dramatically throughout its history. As early as the 15th century it was an important port of call for trading ships from all over Asia. Officially founded in 1602 by Governor Nguyen Phuoc Nguyen, Fai Fo, as it was known then, was to experience 200 years of intense trading, mainly of tea, spices, silk and porcelain. Many merchants set up residences in the town, with living quarters, shop and

A chapel at the Phuc Kien Assembly Hall

SHOPPING IN HOI AN

Hoi An is now famous for its tailoring, as well as for silk. There are outlets every few metres in the old town, while the cloth market has countless traders, often employing children to bring people off the street. Prices are generally lower than in Hanoi or Ho Chi Minh City, and the quality excellent. You can pick out designs that you want copied by leafing through Western catalogues and magazines, and clothes are often ready to be tried on the following day, to make any final adjustments. Shoes can also be made specifically for you, the main outlets centring around Hoang Dieu, near the bridge. Local crafts are booming too, with many workshops doubling as showrooms selling silk lanterns, woodcarvings, pottery and embroidery. The best-known outlet is the Hoi An Handicraft Workshop at 9 Nguyen Hai Hoc.

warehouse all in the same building. Japanese, Chinese and French districts sprang up, while the Dutch, English and Portuguese traded extensively here.

Father Alexandre de Rhodes, famous for Romanising the Vietnamese language, arrived here in 1625, along with the first missionaries. The town went into decline from the late 18th century onwards, due mainly to the silting up of the river, which prevented navigation by large boats. The town's relative unimportance at the time of the French and American Wars is what saved Hoi An from the damage that Hué tragically suffered.

In the town centre
Japanese Covered Bridge
Hoi An's emblem is this simple small bridge of red-painted wood. Its date of

A floating restaurant at Hoi An

construction is thought to be around 1593, when the Japanese community to the west of bridge were tasked with linking their district to the Chinese area to the east of the bridge. Local folklore has it that the bridge was built in an attempt to stop destructive earthquakes that were rocking Japan. The monster said to be carrying the earthquakes was believed to have its heart located in Hoi An, its tail in Japan and head in India. Building a bridge would symbolically drive a sword through the monster's heart. The small temple within the bridge, dedicated to the Taoist god Tran Vo Bac De favoured by sailors, was added later.
Western end of Tran Phu. Museum open daily. Admission charge.

Market
The market seems more in keeping with a traditional country market than a town one. The noise, colour and smells here are intoxicating, and one truly experiences town life in an

authentic setting. A stroll here early in the morning is highly recommended, although you will have to arrive by 6am to enjoy it at its best.

At the back of the market are the ferry docks and the Thu Bon River, which occasionally floods, endangering the first line of shops and restaurants nearest to the water's edge. Here is a good place to try the fresh fish, local soup or fresh bread. Don't be surprised if you are approached by one of the local traders to visit their tailor's shop in the cloth market just next door.
Central market, between Tran Quy Cap, the Cam Nam Bridge and Bach Dang. Open: daily.

Museum of History and Culture
This is perhaps the most interesting of Hoi An's clutch of museums, showing as it does the history of the town using ancient maps and artefacts. The museum sits in a former pagoda, with a peaceful courtyard and attractive carved door panels, and it provides a

FOOD SPECIALITIES IN HOI AN
It is worth trying some of the town's typical local dishes. Here are some of the best known:
Banh Bao ('White Rose'): Steamed manioc-flour parcels of crab and shrimp, with onion-flake topping.
Banh It: A special cake made by steaming green-bean paste and strands of coconut in banana leaves. Triangular parcels of this cake are sold particularly in the market.
Cao Lau: A light soup containing thick noodles, bean sprouts, pork-rind croutons and thin slices of pork, flavoured with mint leaves and star anise.

Fruit and vegetable sellers at Hoi An market

welcome break from shopping in
the busy streets.
*7 Nguyen Hué. Open: daily
8am–5.30pm. Admission charge.*

Phuc Kien Assembly Hall

This is also known as the Fujian
Congregation Hall, because the
Chinese immigrants who lived in this
district of Hoi An hailed from Fujian
in China. Along with other Chinese
enclaves in the town, the Fujian group
maintained its own community centre,
also used as a house of worship. It was
built in 1697 by Chinese mandarins
fleeing to Vietnam after being
overthrown by the Manchu. The
temple is dedicated to the Goddess of
the Sea, Thien Hau Thanh Mau.
Highlights of the Assembly Hall
include the ornately carved wooden
altars in the rear courtyard and the
handsome murals on either side of the

meeting table near the entrance to
the pagoda.
*46 Tran Phu. Open: daily 7am–6pm.
Admission charge.*

Tan Ky House

Hoi An's heritage as a wealthy trading
port has produced many beautifully
restored shop houses. The best known
of these is the Tan Ky House, a well-
preserved late 18th-century example,
typical of its time. It has a narrow
shop front, a very small central
courtyard and access to the river at
the back, from which goods could be
taken upstairs for storage. The house
is charming, with beautifully carved
wood inlaid with mother-of-pearl.
It is sometimes overwhelmed with
visitors, so it is best to come early or
late in the day.
*101 Nguyen Thai Hoc. Open: daily
8am–5.30pm. Admission charge.*

Tran Family House

This ancient family house is famous for the chapel, consisting of three rooms symbolising happiness, prosperity and longevity. The ancestor's altar is looked after by the father of the household. The house was built in 1802 by the civil mandarin Tran Tu Nhac, and was consecrated for the worship of his ancestors. Each year the entire 80-strong family meet at the chapel to venerate their ancestors. If you are lucky, you will be shown around the house, garden and chapel by one of Mr Tran's daughters.

21 Le Loi, at the corner of Phan Chu Trinh. Open: daily 7.30am–6pm. Admission charge.

AROUND HOI AN

One of the pleasant things about the town is the choice of excursions and activities nearby. These include the beaches, islands and Cham ruins.

My Son Cham ruins

The most popular tour from town is to the Cham ruins, 40km (25 miles) southwest of Hoi An, at the foot of Mount My Son (meaning 'Good Mountain'). It is Vietnam's most evocative Cham site and was recently added to UNESCO's list of World Heritage sites. Those who have visited Angkor Wat in Cambodia may be disappointed, but others will find the faded majesty of the ruins and isolated setting most impressive. The atmosphere, however, can tend to get spoiled by coachloads of Vietnamese groups, who chatter noisily and picnic in the grounds.

Rulers of the Cham kingdom were buried here as early as the 4th century according to archaeologists. Kings ruled from the nearby capital of Simhapura, now called Tra Kieu. Most of the ruins standing today were built between the 7th and 13th centuries, with succeeding dynasties adding more and more temples, reaching a total of 70 buildings at its height. The site was the domain of gods and god-kings, supported by groups of servants, priests and dancers who lived on the site. The kings were entrusted with building or restoring a temple during their reign and making offerings to the relevant god.

The ruins were 'discovered' by the French in 1889, when they would have been hidden from view by forests.

Cham site in My Son

During the American War, the Viet Cong based themselves here, which doomed the ruins to relentless bombing by American B52s. Even now, bomb craters around the site are visible, and the surrounding area still contains unexploded mines.

One of the most striking things about the ruins is the impressive masonry skills involved. Instead of mortar, a resin of crushed mollusc shells and crushed bricks was used, meaning that only hairline joins between the bricks are visible. The best-preserved ruins are in Groups B, C and D, labelled so by the French archaeologists who discovered the site in the late 19th century. Sadly, the most impressive building, the magnificent A1 tower, was levelled by bombing.

Group B was the spiritual heart of My Son, with its central *kalan* (tower) being B1, dedicated to the god-king

THE MY LAI MASSACRE

On 16 March 1968 the 11th Infantry Brigade of the American Army received an order to destroy four hamlets suspected of collaborating with the Viet Cong. Although they were met by no resistance, the soldiers, led by Lieutenant William Calley, massacred 504 people, including women and children, and completely destroyed the village. There was only one US casualty, a private who shot himself in the foot rather than take part in the carnage. One year later, participants in the massacre started confessing, and the affair made front-page news. Of the 25 men eventually charged over the massacre, only Lt Calley was found guilty. President Nixon commuted his life sentence of hard labour to house arrest and he was paroled after three years. The mother of one GI lamented 'I gave them a good boy, and they made him a murderer.'

Bhadresvara, built in the 11th century. Only the base of B1 remains, but B5, the repository room, is well worth visiting. The southern façade is well preserved, while the west wall contains an attractive bas-relief depicting a coconut tree entwined by the trunks of two elephants. The chimney-shaped interior would have contained votive offerings (for worshipping the dead) and other objects used for rituals. *40km (25 miles) outhwest of Hoi An. Open: daily 6.30am–4.30pm. Day tours are regularly available from Hoi An. Vehicles are parked near the ticket office, and visitors need to walk across the bridge, where jeeps transport you to within 500m (550 yds) of the site. Admission charge, which includes jeep transportation.*

Cua Dai Beach, near Hoi An

Cua Dai beach

The proximity of the beach to Hoi An is a feature not lost on the growing number of tourists who stay in luxury and mid-range hotels strung along Tran Hung Dao road. Bicycles and motorbikes can easily be hired for a very modest fee, enabling you to enjoy the freedom of the quiet roads out of town.

The beach itself is attractive, with white sands and lots of room for the crowds that flock here at weekends. The main section of the beach is plagued by hawkers. To avoid this, either move further down the beach or hire a deckchair and umbrella at one of the café-restaurants along the beach. Some of the resort hotels such as the Hoi An Beach Resort have quiet private beaches which you can use for a fee.

4km (2¹/2 miles) east of Hoi An town. Just follow Tran Hung Dao out of town. If you arrive by bicycle or motorbike, you will have to leave it at the regulated parking site a few hundred metres from the beach, for a small fee.

SON MY VILLAGE

Not to be confused with My Son, the location for the Cham towers near Hoi An, this village is more infamously known as My Lai (*see opposite*), scene of one of the most horrific episodes of the American War. In fact, the location of this village in an area far from other tourist sites ensures that it receives only a trickle of visitors, who make a special visit to it, often due to some connection with the war.

The Son My Memorial Park is located in Tu Cung, a nearby sub-hamlet, with statues remembering that fateful day. There are two buildings, with a plaque recording the names of those killed, and a museum containing photographs taken by the American army photographer, located at the spot where the worst-hit hamlet stood.

12km (7 miles) east of Quang Ngai, which is 130km (81 miles) south of Danang. The site is open daily 7am–5pm. Admission charge.

Boats on an inlet near Cua Dai

Walk: Around Hoi An

This walk covers the main section of the old centre, taking you by the river and through the narrow streets, stopping off to visit the most attractive places of interest. The walk is best done as early as possible in the morning, when the market is at its most interesting.

Allow 2 hours (plus time in places of interest and food and drink stops).

Start at the Central Market on Nguyen Duy Hieu, where stalls selling fruit and vegetables, snacks and drinks congregate. There is a ticket office a few metres heading west along Tran Phu where you can buy the Hoi An tourist ticket that allows you to visit most of the town's sights (see p97).

1 Central Market

A stroll around the market in the morning is a great way to see the townspeople at their most energetic. Fresh produce, especially fish caught in the early hours of the morning, is carried and displayed, and the market is full of bustle and colour. The market is an ideal place for breakfast, which typically is a bowl of noodle soup (*pho*) for the locals. *Walk west along Tran Phu for a few metres and you will see a grand, pink, triple-arched gate on your right at No 46.*

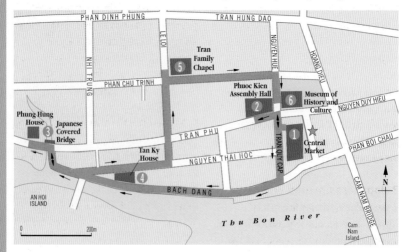

An ancestral altar in the Tran Family Chapel

2 Phuoc Kien Assembly Hall

The spacious flowered terrace is thankfully shaded from the sun, and you will see handsome murals near the pagoda entrance, depicting a battle between the Manchu and the Ming in China. The Ming mandarins subsequently fled to Vietnam, helping to set up this assembly hall for the Kien people (*see p100*).

Head back to the market, but take Tran Quy Cap running south to the river. At the river, you will see Cam Nam Bridge on your left. Turn right instead, keeping the ferry station on your left. Bach Dang street is full of restaurants and cafés, and is an ideal place to succumb to the temptations of the waiters calling for your custom, and have a drink. Continue along Bach Dang as the road bends right.

3 Japanese Covered Bridge

This bridge is diminutive but an important symbol of the town. It was an important crossing point over the muddy creek, linking the Japanese district in the west to the Chinese area in the east.

Retrace your footsteps along the river, but bear left at the little square where local festivities take place, at the beginning of Nguyen Thai Hoc street. Look for No 101 on your right.

4 Tan Ky House

One of the town's most prized architectural gems is this ancient Chinese house (*see p100*), the first to be declared an Historic Monument, in 1985.

Continue along Nguyen Thai Hoc and turn left at the junction with Le Loi. Walk north for a block until the next junction with Phan Chu Trinh, looking for a walled compound on your right.

5 Tran Family Chapel

If you are lucky, you will be welcomed by one of the daughters of Mr Tran and treated to lotus-flower tea and sugared coconut in one of the pretty flowered gardens. The house has been kept within the family for 300 years (*see p101*).

Turn right and walk eastwards along Phan Chu Trinh, and turn right onto Nguyen Hué. A few metres down, look left.

6 Museum of History and Culture

This former pagoda (*see p99*) contains a peaceful courtyard, an ideal place to end the tour. It is only a few metres north of the Central Market. The small museum contains fascinating maps of Fai Fo, as the town was called, and artefacts from Hoi An's colourful history.

South central Vietnam

This region of Vietnam exemplifies the rich diversity of geography and attractions in the country but is often neglected by tourists. The Central and Southern Highlands offer rich experiences off the beaten track, enabling you to meet fascinating hill-tribe people in their traditional villages, visit superb national parks and experience stunning natural beauty. Beach and water-sports lovers need look no further than the resort-town of Nha Trang. In contrast, Dalat is a highly popular hill-station area, with crisp, clean air, alpine scenery and delicious garden vegetables.

DALAT

Vietnam's premier hill station is located among the hills of the Lang Bian plateau in the Southern Highlands. It was a favourite destination of French colonials seeking a cool climate away from the heat of the lowlands; their successors are its Vietnamese honeymooners, homesick European expats and Ho Chi Minh City's nouveaux riches.

Many travellers are disappointed with Dalat, mainly because it can get very busy with tourists, but also because it offers little new to many foreigners used to pleasant country air and pretty scenery. Many of the tourist attractions have a kitsch style that reflects Vietnamese taste but which can look gaudy. However, if you can see past these flaws, Dalat offers pretty lakes, waterfalls and pine forests, and a refreshingly cool climate.

Dalat first caught the attention of Dr Alexandre Yersin (*see box on p114*) in 1893 when he discovered the therapeutic properties of the climate on an exploratory mission into the Southern Highlands. Four years later, a hill station was built to cater for convalescing or stressed French *colons* (colonials). The city was spared the bombing of the American War, and so has remained relatively unchanged for the past 50 years.

Dalat town

The town is dominated by Lake Xuan Huong and surrounded by hills, creating a charming setting. The lake is a great favourite for Vietnamese couples and families, who hire swan-shaped pedal boats to row on the lake. The northern shore of the lake is the most lively and built-up part of town, with winding roads and long flights of steps to negotiate the hills. At the end of Nguyen Thi Minh Khai is the main market, housed in an ugly, depressing concrete block of a building. It is worth a stroll around to admire the incredible range of locally grown flowers, fruit and vegetables, many of which are unavailable elsewhere in Vietnam.

Overlooking the lake from the south is the gorgeous Sofitel Dalat Palace hotel, a gem of colonial architecture. A stroll in the gardens running down to the lake and tea in its luxurious lounges is a treat worth the expense. Across the

South central Vietnam

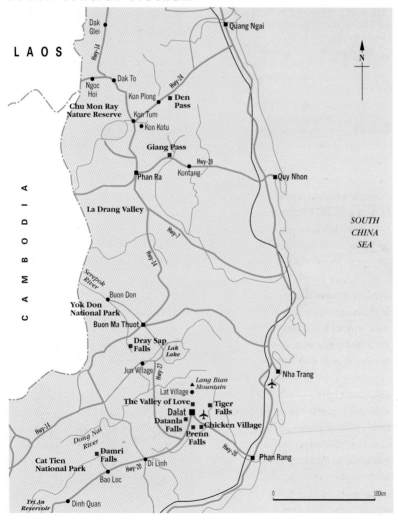

THE REAL-LIFE KURTZ

Those familiar with Joseph Conrad's novel *Heart of Darkness*, later adapted into the film *Apocalypse Now* by Francis Ford Coppola, will know the character Kurtz, played by Marlon Brando in the film. A real-life version of the character existed in the late 1900s.

A French rogue named Marie-David de Mayrena arrived among the Sedang people and proclaimed himself King Marie I. He adopted a constitution and a flag, and tried to gain recognition for his position.

Mayrena spent several days in the Continental Hotel in Saigon with an array of courtiers, and moved out without paying, after decorating the hotel manager with the title of 'National Order of the Kingdom of the Sedangs'. His attempts to make financial gain from his fictitious position came to nothing, and he died penniless in Malaysia from a snakebite.

road is the pink Cathedral, with its 47m- (154ft) high bell tower. Built in 1931 and dedicated to St Nicholas, it has lovely stained-glass windows, imported from France.

Bao Dai Summer Palace

This is a refreshing change from the usual style of Vietnamese royal palace. The architecture of the building, begun in 1933, as well as the interior style, is very much Western 1940s and '50s elegance, combined with Eastern luxury. The palace was built to give Emperor Bao Dai a summer retreat where he could enjoy the cool mountain air and indulge in his favourite pastime of hunting. It does not have the stuffy, historic feel of some museums, and one can imagine the royal family living in this mustard-coloured building and strolling around the pine gardens.

Le Hong Pong, which is 500m (550 yds) west of the cathedral. Open: daily 7am–5.30pm. Admission charge.

Hang Nga's Crazy House

Another popular stop on many city-tours is this 'Crazy House'. It is the work of the daughter of the Communist Party leader who succeeded Ho Chi Minh, which she designed on her return to Dalat after studying architecture in Moscow. It is a mixture of spider's web and sandcastle, a fun building that seems totally impractical for its use as a working guesthouse.

3 Huynh Thuc Khang. Tel: (063) 822070. Open: daily. Admission charge.

AROUND DALAT

Outside of the town are several sights worth visiting. The surrounding

Bao Dai Palace, Dalat

countryside is very pretty and well worth making a trip out to see. The waterfalls in the area are best seen in the wet season, as they don't look so impressive during the dry season (December–May).

Tiger Falls

Out of the many falls in the area, this is the most impressive, even in the dry season. You need to climb down a concrete stairway from the restaurants at the top to the base of the falls. It is popular with locals, who come here to sit on the boulders at the bottom and picnic.

11km (7 miles) northeast of Dalat, beyond Trai Mat Village. Open: daily 7.30am–5pm. Admission charge.

The Valley of Love (Thung Lung Tinh Yeu)

Thung Lung Tinh Yeu is located 5km (3 miles) north of town, with some kitsch diversions aimed at locals, around an artificial lake.

Along Phu Dong Thien Vuong. Open: daily 7am–5pm. Admission charge.

Chicken Village (Lang Con Ca)

Lang Con Ca is famous for its giant concrete statue of a chicken in the middle of the village. There are several theories as to its meaning. One story is that a bride-to-be went into the mountains to search for a chicken with nine toes, following the demands of the groom's family for a special present.

She died tragically in the mountains, and the locals asked the government to build this memorial in commemoration of the young girl. The local minority people, the Koho, are skilled at making textiles using unusually operated looms.

18km (11 miles) south of Dalat, just west of Highway 20.

THE CENTRAL HIGHLANDS

The Central Highlands do not receive the same number of visitors as destinations on the coastal tourist route, or for that matter even Dalat. This is a shame, as the area has some of the most stunning scenery in the country, and some fascinating ethnic communities.

The Highlands remained out of bounds for foreigners until the 1990s. Even then, the area was slow to build up sufficient tourist facilities to attract many visitors. Now there is a steady improvement in both accommodation and transport. The ethnic minorities who live there have themselves had a tough time of it. There have been political issues regarding land rights and freedom of worship, but hopefully these will be resolved as tourist interest in the area grows. The villages struggle to subsist on the fruits of the land, although ever-expanding coffee, tea and cotton plantations are boosting the local economy.

In the high season, tour groups visit the Highlands from Danang, Hoi An, Nha Trang and of course Dalat, although visits can be arranged once you travel to the main towns in the area: Kon Tum, Pleiku and Buon Ma Thuot. While the towns themselves have little of interest, they are good bases from which to explore the landscape and ethnic minorities around it. Generally, foreigners need to have a guide to explore the minority villages.

Around Kon Tum

Kon Tum is the capital of the province of the same name, a pleasant town in an attractive setting, and with a mild climate. In the area, the key minority groups are the Sedang and Ba Na (also spelt Bahnar), and to a lesser extent the Gia Rai.

The area has a strong Christian influence upon it. The first Christians arrived in 1851 under the leadership of Father Dourisboure, and many of the Ba Na were converted, with the encouragement of the French colonial rulers. Remnants of the era remain, such as the whitewashed Tan Huong Church and a restored wooden church nearby.

Also worth visiting is the suspension bridge over the Dakbla River, a great place to watch the wonderful red sunset.

Chu Mon Ray Nature Reserve

Virgin forest, extending to about 50,000 hectares (123,553 acres), covers this mountainous region very near the Cambodian border. With a guide it is possible to see rare monkeys and other endangered species. Mount Chu Mon Ray itself can be climbed, but ask at the Kon Tum tourist office for details of

E DE CUSTOMS

The E De are mainly hunter-gatherers but are famed for their elephant taming. The basis of the E De culture is a matriarchal social system. This entails the groom taking the bride's name, living with her family, and if necessary, marrying her youngest sister if his wife dies. The oldest man in the village usually becomes the head of the village, wearing jewellery such as earrings made from elephant tusks. The E De traditionally eat with their hands rather than using implements like chopsticks. Upon death, they are buried vertically in a hollow tree section, with a bamboo pipe above ground to enable the villagers to push down food and drink to the deceased.

organised walks. There are several villages of the Gia Rai minority, the best known being Plei Chot. Here you will see their traditional skills of basket making and weaving. If you are lucky, you will observe the ceremony of 'the passing of the river', in which rice wine in a jar is drunk through a straw, until a bamboo stick inside floats to the surface. Nearby the village is a fascinating cemetery with eerie wooden statues, with diverse representations including elephant tusks to ward off evil spirits, Joan of Arc and, strangely, French Marshal Leclerc.
30km (19 miles) west of Kon Tum, beyond Lake Yaly.

Kon Kotu Village

This lovely village is set in a wonderful wooded area by the river. It is reached by driving past stilt villages, cassava- and sugar-cane plantations and

crossing the bridge at Kon Klor. Try to see the superb *rong* (communal house) just by the suspension bridge. It is possible to stay overnight in the *rong* in the middle of the village among the friendly Ba Na people. This lofty communal house, with a thatched roof and bamboo wall and floors, was built using no nails. Remember to ask permission before entering a family's house and to show common courtesy to the villagers.
3km (2 miles) east of Kon Tum, following the Tran Hung Dao out from Kon Tum.

In and around Buon Ma Thuot
The main ethnic minorities around here are the E De and the M'nong. They can be visited in several key villages, including Ako Dhong and Buon Don. Other attractions in the area include an array of stunning waterfalls, the country's largest wildlife reserve at Yok Don National Park, and the beauty of Lak Lake. Don't forget that the area is the heart of Vietnam's coffee industry, so make sure that you sample the product at one of the many cafés in the town or surrounding villages.

Dray Sap Falls
The most popular waterfall in the area is this one, sitting side by side with the Dray Nur Falls. Dray Sap is crescent-shaped, with violent explosions of splash and spray that can be glimpsed from the suspension bridge near the car park. Measuring 15m (49ft) high and 100m (328ft) wide, it isn't surprising to

hear that the name means 'waterfall of smoke'. You can walk around the river in front of the falls, then walk up to the right of the falls, to some flat rocks that nudge the torrent of water at the top.
5km (3 miles) down the road from Cut Dut, off the RN14 road southwest of Buon Ma Thuot. Admission charge. The falls can get crowded at weekends, so a weekday visit is recommended.

Lak Lake
This is one of the area's most popular natural attractions. It sits at the bottom of a wide crater surrounded by extinct volcanoes. Jun Village is situated on the edge of the lake, on a very small peninsula of bamboo groves. Here, the several hundred M'nong people live in longhouses on stilts. Tourists have become so common here that the children seem uninterested in foreigners, and there is a rather tacky souvenir shop in the village. Elephant rides are available, although they are relatively expensive here compared to other sites in the area.
56km (35 miles) southeast of Buon Ma Thuot off the RN27 road.

Yok Don National Park
Vietnam's largest wildlife reserve covers 115,000 hectares (284,171 acres), very near the border with Cambodia and the Serepok River. It is home to tigers, leopards and bears, as well as 60 other types of animal and 450 types of bird. However, most are secluded in a no-go
Continued on p114

Bamboo

'Beautiful bamboo trees growing by the pool … Beautiful bamboo trees growing by the village temple.' In his folk song *Beautiful Bamboo Trees*, Van Nguyen presented bamboo as a symbol of peace. Songs that once served only to reflect the history of quaint villages with wooden bridges and bamboo-encircled ponds took on new meanings in times of upheaval and war as a way of symbolising and helping preserve the simplicity of traditional Vietnamese life.

Bamboo has been tied to Vietnamese people's daily life for thousands of years, being described as 'brother' in Vietnamese. Even now

A stand of bamboo

you will see it used in hundreds of ways. Its symbolic importance was not lost on Ho Chi Minh, whose mausoleum is flanked on both sides by clusters of bamboo trees. Bamboo has become so much a part of the culture and memory of societies in this part of the world that the existence of an archaeological Bamboo Age has not been ruled out. Its use in food and cooking goes far back in time.

Bamboo is the most diverse group of plants in the grass family, and the most primitive sub-family. It is distinguished by woody stems, a robust nature and infrequent flowering. A single bamboo clump can produce up to 15km (19 miles) of usable pole in its lifetime. It is also very adaptable, with some species being deciduous and others evergreen. Bamboo grows and develops well in every terrain, from high mountains and hill slopes to river and spring banks and plains. It has minimal environmental impact since it can be harvested after three years of growth in controlled forests. The grass' potential for checking soil erosion and for road embankment stabilisation is being increasingly recognised. It is equally important for providing fast

Panels of woven split bamboo, used in buildings

vegetative cover to deforested areas. Throughout rural Asia it is used for building bridges and as scaffoldings in construction projects.

Bamboo is still highly popular because of its strength, natural beauty and multifaceted utility. There are about 1,500 documented traditional uses for it, from cradle to coffin. It supplies raw material for housing, mats, blinds, furniture, ladders, fencing, banana props, containers, pipes, toys, musical instruments, handicrafts, toothpicks, chopsticks, raw material for pulp and paper, and even food in the form of bamboo shoots. The leaves are very nutritious, so feeding them to livestock creates no waste in the system.

Bamboo clumps can be quite dense

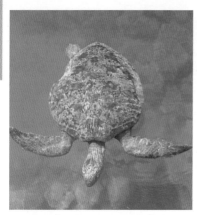

A turtle near Tri Nguyen Island, Nha Trang

zone for tourists. Safaris can be organised by the park headquarters, especially in the dry season when Yok Don Mountain is full of wildlife searching for food and water. Elephant rides are the most popular activity in the park and can easily be arranged. *45km (28 miles) northwest of Buon Ma Thuot. Admission charge. Simple accommodation is available from the Park HQ.*

Buon Don Village

A stay in this village, very near the headquarters of the Yok Don park, is highly recommended. It is the centre of the country's elephant breeding programme, with elephant rides available around the surrounding forests and Serepok River. The E De ethnic minority here have a proud tradition of capturing and rearing wild elephants. Longhouses that have been adapted for Western tourists are available for the night.

NHA TRANG

This is primarily a seaside destination, ideal for chilling out on attractive beaches, doing some snorkelling or diving, or visiting the outlying islands off the coast. There are some sights, such as the Cham towers at Po Nagar, but this is essentially a place to relax and recharge your batteries.

The coastal town has a completely different feel to other places in Vietnam. As soon as you arrive, you feel the town's pace a little slower, starting with the easy-going taxi drivers at the airport who offer to take you round a selection of hotels. Much development work has taken place in recent years, so that the main focus of the beach-front has moved southwards over the years.

ALEXANDRE YERSIN

This famous adopted son of Nha Trang was a leading French-Swiss bacteriologist who spent most of his life exploring the Orient, starting out as a ship's doctor. He settled in Nha Trang in 1895, introducing quinine and rubber-producing trees to the area, as part of his laboratory development, which was to become the famous Pasteur Institute. His claims to fame include his discovery of the microbe responsible for the bubonic plague, discovering Dalat, which became one of Vietnam's leading hill-stations, and his ability to predict typhoons, which saved the lives of fishermen. He also did valuable educational work in sanitation and agriculture. The respect in which the Vietnamese hold him is reflected in his description as 'the revered humanist and benefactor of the Vietnamese people', and in the tomb to him built nearby by the town's fishermen.

Note that from October to December the sea is choppy and the water becomes murky – not the best time for swimming, snorkelling or diving.

Nha Trang town

The main area for travellers is Biet Thu street, full of good-value hotels, restaurants and bars. Cho Dam (central market) is the centre of the downtown area, lively and colourful. As you go north towards the Cham towers (*see p116*), you pass the large, scenic fishing port. Although the town isn't very big, you can avoid long walks up and down the beach by hiring a bicycle or motorbike at low cost.

Alexandre Yersin Museum

This handsome residence next to the Pasteur Institute (*see opposite*) tells the story of the scientist's life and work. Among the interesting artefacts on display are barometers, telescopes, and a huge library that reflects his unquenchable thirst for knowledge. The laboratory he set up was to become the Pasteur Institute in 1903, and it is still operational today.
10 Tran Phu. Tel: (058) 829540. Open: Mon–Sat 8–11am & 2–4.30pm. Admission charge.

The beach

This municipal beach is the best in Vietnam, over 6km (4 miles) long and consisting of soft yellow sand and rolling waves. The main section of the beach is between the War Memorial and the Pasteur Institute to the north of the town. However, there are lots of hawkers roaming the beach, selling everything from T-shirts to massages.

For more peace and quiet, head to the southern end. North of the Ana Mandara Resort is a well-organised water park, and just south are some beach-front restaurants offering free use of sun loungers.

The Louisiana Café at the southern end of Tran Phu is another place that offers privacy on its beach in exchange for patronising its bar and restaurant.

Around Nha Trang

Nha Trang attracts many scuba-divers to its shores, as it is the dive-centre of Vietnam. Water-lovers will enjoy the range of water sports on offer, including parasailing, jet-skiing and of course snorkelling. For the rest, there are lots of other attractions around the town, as evidenced by the number of day-trips advertised by the numerous tour offices in town.

The islands

Perhaps the most popular day-trip is to the islands that dot the bay. Trips often include lunch, use of rubber rings to float and drink cocktails in, a fruit-tasting party and snorkelling. Alternatively, chartered boats can be organised.

Hon Mieu island is the nearest to Nha Trang, and contains a colourful fishing village at Tri Nguyen and an outdoor aquarium. Other popular

Po Nagar Cham Towers, Nha Trang

islands include Hon Tam, Hon Tre
(Bamboo Island) and Hon Lao
(Monkey Island).

Po Nagar Cham Towers
These intriguing towers look impressive
from afar, perched on a hillside
overlooking the fishing bay of Nha
Trang. They were built sometime
around the 10th century and have
deteriorated badly over the years.
In the days of the Cham empire,
Nha Trang was known as Eatrang
('river of reeds').

Out of the four towers remaining
from the original ten, the most
impressive is the northern tower, built
in 817 and 23m (75ft) high. The lotus-
petal motifs and the Shiva figures over
the door are original, while other
sections have been heavily restored.

The boulders just behind the towers
are worth climbing, as they afford great
views over the Cai River to the town.

*1.5km (1 mile) north of Nha Trang city
centre. Open: daily 6am–6pm.
Admission charge.*

Thap Ba Hot Springs
This natural spa complex is gaining
popularity with visitors who want to
pamper themselves with natural
treatments and mud baths. This is
often the last destination in 'River-trip'
day-tours out of Nha Trang, and a
stress-relieving experience. There is
a range of treatments on offer, with
a mud bath being the most popular.
Floating in a clammy bath of mud is
a strangely therapeutic experience,
and there are plenty of hot showers to
rinse the slime off afterwards. The
waters here are rich in sodium chloride
and are considered beneficial for all
sorts of ailments.
*Just north of the Cham Towers on a road
heading west. Tel: (058) 835287. Prices
vary according to treatments selected.*

MUI NE

This used to be a sleepy quiet backwater, but its growing popularity with expats and wealthy locals from Ho Chi Minh City is driving the development of up-market beach hotels and better tourist facilities.

It is a quiet version of Nha Trang, with a narrower beach and fewer facilities, but just right for tourists who want some seclusion and simplicity. Its popularity seems to stem from the 1990s, when Mui Ne fortuitously became the optimum spot to view the eclipse of the sun. As a result of this exposure, the place has become one of the fastest-growing beach destinations in Vietnam, with a choice of up-market hotel resorts and backpacker hotels.

The main activities here are relaxing on the beach, windsurfing and kite-surfing. The 'Jibes' resort seems to be the place to take part in these activities. Sightseeing is limited, although the fishing village and its picturesque bay are worth visiting, and offer lots of photo opportunities. Just out of town are famous red-coloured sand dunes, set in a very unusual location inland, overlooking the sea. Some dunes are exceptionally high and ideal for sliding down on simple toboggans, enthusiastically hired out by local children.

South central coast

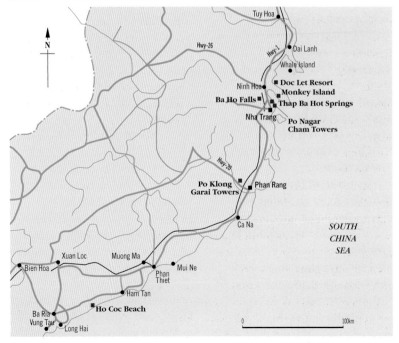

Ho Chi Minh City

This is the economic powerhouse of Vietnam, a huge, sprawling metropolis full of energy, commerce and sheer ambition. Here you will find reams of top-notch restaurants and hotels, luxury shops and all the nightlife you can handle. There is a few days' worth of sightseeing to be done in the city, with museums, temples and historical sites from its colourful past, and architecture that reflects its mix of modern, colonial and Asian cultures.

Tourists arriving here will experience sensory overload, with too many people, motorbikes and frenzied street activity for some Western sensibilities. In a short time, though, most succumb to the spirit and warmth of the city and its inhabitants.

Often abbreviated to 'HCM City', the full name is Thanh Pho Ho Chi Minh, although for many people the city will always be 'Saigon'. Economic growth in the city is breathtaking, with office blocks and hotels rising out of the ground at logic-defying speed.

HCM is divided into 18 districts. Visitors mostly keep to Districts One (the central area), Three and Five. Many visitors do not venture out of District One, which contains most of interest to the tourist, including the old French colonial quarter. However, there are a few sights worth seeing outside of this district, most notably Cholon, the Chinese Quarter.

The key to enjoying the city is not to rush – the heat and bustle of the streets will soon take their toll. Break up day-trips and sightseeing with downtime, relaxing in pagodas, parks, cafés and restaurants. The inhabitants of HCM City are friendlier, warmer and more easy-going than their Northern counterparts. However, the city has a few more annoyances, such as bag-snatching or pickpocketing, particularly prevalent in the Dong Khoi area and Ben Thanh Market.

History

The area had humble origins as a sleepy fishing backwater, a combination of forest, swampland and waterways. By the 17th century the city of Prei Nokor was a strong trading hub that drew the attention of the Viet empire-builders. The Nguyen Dynasty gave the city the name Saigon, thought to be derived from the Vietnamese word for the kapok tree. The city became the capital of Nguyen Anh, who built a walled fortress, the Gia Dinh Citadel, in the late 18th century, to protect it from the Tay Son rebellion.

The French, who had long coveted the city, used the pretext of the Emperor's persecution of French missionaries to seize Saigon in 1861. The city became the capital of French Cocochina upon the Treaty of Saigon in 1862. Many of the colonial buildings in the city were built in this 'golden age', including the Cathedral, Post Office and Governor's Palace, using the huge profits made from exporting Vietnam's rubber and rice.

After occupation by the Japanese in World War II the city was briefly ruled by the British, who promptly handed it back to the French. This sparked the French War, ending in 1954, with Saigon becoming the capital of South Vietnam. Under President Diem and during the American War, Saigon was bankrolled by the Americans, who used the city as a playground for resting GIs and administrators. Sleazy bars were strung along Dong Khoi street and the Vietnamese developed their commercial flair from these gravy-train years. It is estimated that there were 56,000 prostitutes in the city at this time. When the Americans left in 1975, the economy collapsed.

The newly arrived Communists renamed Saigon 'Ho Chi Minh City' in 1975, heralding a new chapter of austerity that only ended in the 1990s

Ho Chi Minh City

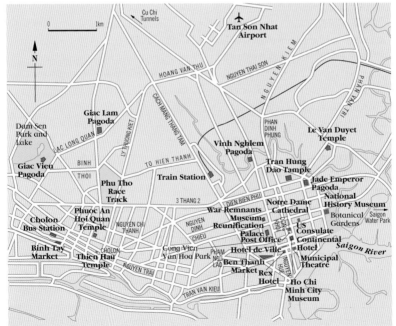

with the opening up of the economy to capitalist ideas. The city is now more like the old American pre-1975 Saigon, with its pulsating nightlife and outright commercialism, than the post-1975 Communist-governed austerity. As Henry Kamm of the *New York Times* observed, 'The southern metropolis has cast off the dour sackcloth the victor forced it to wear. That it has been able to do so with such aplomb is not really surprising. The hair shirt never fit.'

DISTRICT ONE

District One is the central part of the city, containing most of the main sights, as well as being the location for travellers' accommodation and shopping. The Saigon River borders this area to the east and southeast, while the Botanical Gardens forms the northeast edge, and the Cong Vien Van Hoa park (Municipal Cultural park) roughly the western border. Many locals and expats still refer to District One as 'Saigon'.

District One can be divided into specific areas, based around cultural sights or streets. Dong Khoi is perhaps the most famous street in the city, for it epitomises the French colonial era in not only its sights and architecture, but also its classy boutiques, restaurants and bars. Nguyen Hue is also in the French Quarter, in fact running parallel to Dong Khoi, from the river to the old Hotel de Ville. The Reunification Palace is in the middle of an area with a range of places of interest, from museums to the peaceful Cong Vien Van Hoa park.

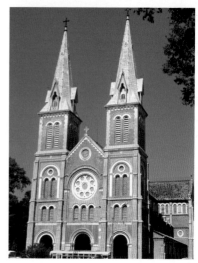

Notre Dame Cathedral

The final area worth noting in District One is Pham Ngu Lao, the backpacker district. It is full of cheap guesthouses, restaurants and internet cafés, located southeast of District One.

Dong Khoi

This famous street has a rich and varied history, and consequently contains many places of interest, as well as being an ideal place to stroll around, among the sophisticated restaurants and shops. Dong Khoi starts at the Saigon River and shoots northwest, ending at the Cathedral and Post Office.

During French colonial times, this street was called Rue Catinat, and then Tu Do (Freedom) in the American era, when the street was a notorious red-light district. In 1975, it was renamed Dong Khoi, meaning 'General Uprising', a suitably Communist name.

Continental Hotel

This historic hotel is well worth looking into, to savour the colonial atmosphere of the central courtyard, which also displays some fascinating old photos from the hotel's archives. Much of the action in Graham Greene's novel *The Quiet American* is set in the hotel in the 1950s. It was built in 1880, the bastion of French high society, and later became the press headquarters during the American War.
132–134 Dong Khoi. Tel: (08) 829 9201. www.continentalvietnam.com

Municipal Theatre

This lovingly restored building is at its best at night, standing grandly, looking eastwards down Le Loi street. Built in 1899, it was temporarily used by the South Vietnamese National Assembly from 1955 to 1975. Its steps are now popular with young couples, who sit and gaze at the neon lights of the area, and the steady stream of motorbikes that cruise down Dong Khoi. Cultural events are still held here, including music and dance shows. Keep a look-out for the banners that hang outside the theatre.
At the corner of Le Loi and Dong Khoi.

Notre Dame Cathedral

The two graceful spires of this red-brick cathedral have been unfairly described as 'the ears of a hidden jack rabbit'. It was built in 1880 and has pretty stained-glass windows. It is a popular location for newly weds to be photographed, especially in the park in front, which contains a statue of the Virgin Mary.
Paris Commune Square (Cong Xa Paris). Open: daily 7–11am, 3–4pm. Daily services at 5.30am and 5.00pm, with seven services on Sun.

Post office

At first glance, one could be forgiven for mistaking this grand building for a 19th-century railway station. The superb arched metallic roof, built in 1891, was designed by Gustave Eiffel. It is worth looking inside, if only to admire the huge portrait of Ho Chi Minh on the back wall and the old wooden tables and benches still used by the post office staff. Visitors who wish to send parcels and packages abroad should walk around the back to the international parcel dispatch office.
Dong Khoi. Open: Mon–Sat 6am–10pm. International Parcel Dispatch is open Mon–Fri 7.30am–noon, 1–4pm, at Hai Ba Trung.

Around Nguyen Hue

The French colonial administrators would be turning in their graves if they saw Nguyen Hue street now, filled with *xe om*, a modern, unglamorous street of shopping malls and souvenir shops. It was once a filled-in canal developed by the French into a replica of a tree-lined Parisian avenue known as Charner Boulevard, the 'Champs Elysées of the East'. It runs parallel to Dong Khoi, from the river to the former town hall, the Hotel de Ville.

Ho Chi Minh City Museum

This grand white building has a rich and varied history of its own, and is well worth visiting to see one of the most diverse and interesting exhibitions in the city. It illustrates the history of HCM City, focusing primarily on the people's struggle in the wars against the French and Americans. Most eye-catching is the selection of military hardware in the gardens, from US helicopters and fighter planes to Soviet tanks. Inside there are some fascinating displays showing the ingenuity of the Vietnamese people in times of oppression, for example the fishing boat with a double bottom used to secrete arms.

The building began life in 1886 as the residence of the Governor of Cocochina, known as Gia Long Palace. President Diem lived here in 1962 after his former residence was bombed in an assassination attempt. He was later to hide in the tunnels underneath this building before fleeing to Cholon, where he was subsequently captured and shot.

65 Ly Tu Trong. Tel: (08) 829 9741.
Open: daily 8am–4pm. Admission charge.

Hotel de Ville

It is ironic to see this ostentatious colonial city hall, a symbol of triumphant imperialism, flying the red Vietnamese flag, now the People's Committee headquarters. An impressive sculpture showing Ho Chi Minh with a child looks down the avenue from the park in front of the

THE GATES OF THE PRESIDENTIAL PALACE

On 30 April 1975 the palace was the setting for one of the most dramatic scenes of the American War, covered by photographers and reporters as Saigon, the capital of South Vietnam, fell to the Communist army. A Viet Cong tank rammed the gates of the palace in one of the defining moments of the war. English journalist James Fenton, who hitched a ride on the tank itself, wrote: 'The tank backed again, and I observed a man with a nervous smile opening the centre portion of the gate. We drove into the grounds of the palace and fired a salute.' Inside, President Duong Van Minh was waiting to surrender. He evidently said to General Bui Tin 'I have been waiting since early this morning to transfer power to you.' The General replied 'Your power has crumbled. You cannot give up what you do not have.'

building. The 'cream puff' style of architecture is somewhat incongruous in this modern city, with Corinthian columns, a long yellow façade and a high belfry tower. Built in 1908, it was originally the city's administration centre and is now one of its symbols. At night, the building is beautifully lit. *Thanh Ton.*

Rex Hotel

This famous hotel has stunning views from its rooftop garden terrace, one of the best bars to visit at night. It may appear a historic hotel, but it was only converted to its present use in 1976. The building was originally a garage for the Renaults and Peugeots of the French expat community, and then became a business centre in 1959. In the 1960s it

hosted regular press briefing sessions on the war against Communism.
141 Nguyen Hue. Tel: (08) 829 2185.
www.rexhotelvietnam.com

The Reunification Palace

Taking a guided tour through this former South Vietnamese government HQ is like going back to the 1960s and '70s. The décor is understated kitsch, with airy banqueting rooms, marble galleries and elegant reception rooms. The building was finished in 1966, replacing Diem's presidential palace.
Entrances on Nam Ky Khoi Nghia and Nguyen Du. Tel: (08) 822 3652. Open: daily 7.30–11.30am and 1.30–4.30pm. Admission charge includes a guided tour.

Cong Vien Van Hoa Park

This huge park is pleasant to walk in to get away from city life, and there are plenty of opportunities for people-watching. The Workers Sports Club, formerly the 'Cercle Sportif', has an array of sporting facilities: tennis for the well-heeled of the city, basketball and badminton for teenagers, and a large open-air swimming pool popular with expats, tourists and school groups. The Cercle Sportif in its day was a hub of French expat society into which only Westerners were allowed. The clubhouse is still attractively grand.
The park adjoins the northwestern edge of the Reunification Palace. The Workers Sports Club is at the park's northern corner, with an entrance on Nguyen Thi Minh Khai. Swimming is available to foreigners for a modest charge.

War Remnants Museum

One block away is the city's most popular museum, exhibiting the history of the French and American Wars in all their shocking and depressing detail. Those with a sensitive disposition will find the photographs of mutilation and death particularly unpalatable. It was formerly called the 'War Crimes Museum' and was bitterly anti-French and anti-American in tone. It is less one-sided now, although it is difficult to remain neutral when faced with the depiction of modern warfare and its tools.
28 Vo Van Tran. Tel: (08) 829 5587. Open: daily 7.30–11.45am and 1.30–5.15pm. Admission charge.

Inside the Reunification Palace, HCM City

Uncle Ho

'Uncle Ho' (Bac Ho), as Ho Chi Minh is affectionately known, was Vietnam's greatest leader, helping to rid the country of the French colonial rulers and establishing an independent country. Sadly, he did not live to see the North and South reunified after the American War, dying in 1969.

Born in 1890, Nguyen Sinh Cung was the youngest child of a mandarin who was dismissed from the imperial court in Hué for anti-colonialist sympathies. He attended high school in Hué and was expelled for taking part in a student protest. He left Vietnam aged 21 on a steamship bound for France, and travelled extensively in North America, Africa and Europe. His various jobs included spells in the dockyards in New York, as a pastry chef in London, and a

A poster of Ho Chi Minh from the time of his nationalist struggle

photographic retoucher in Paris. In France, he took the name Nguyen Ai Quoc (Nguyen the Patriot), learned several languages and became active in debating the issue of Indochinese independence.

During the 1919 Versailles Peace Conference at the end of World War I, Ho caused a stir by publishing a petition demanding independence for Vietnam. He was inspired by Lenin's opposition to imperialism around the world, and helped to found the French Communist Party in 1920.

Three years later he was hired by the Communist International organisation in Moscow, and posted to China as an agent, setting up the Revolutionary Youth League of Vietnam, a precursor to the Vietnamese Communist Party, which he founded in 1930 in Hong Kong. He escaped arrest by the authorities a number of times, but was imprisoned in Hong Kong before escaping with the help of prison hospital staff.

In 1941 he returned to Vietnam for the first time in 30 years, suffering from dysentery, malaria and tuberculosis. Now aged 51 and known as Ho Chi Minh (meaning 'He Who Enlightens'), he was still a

Statue of Uncle Ho in HCM City

control, and Ho Chi Minh wrote Vietnam's Declaration of Independence, reading it from the balcony of Hanoi's Opera House in August 1945 (see p11).

He was forced to flee Hanoi when the French seized power again soon afterwards, but led the guerrilla war against the colonialists, which ended at the historic battle of Dien Bien Phu in 1954. Following independence, he was expected to move into the Presidential Palace in Hanoi, formerly the French Governor of Indochina's residence. Always a modest man, he chose instead to live first in the gardener's house in the same grounds and then in a wooden stilt house which he had built a year later (see p54). He ruled as President of the Democratic Republic of Vietnam for 15 years, his health slowly deteriorating. By 1969, his heart began to fail, and he died on 2 September, now Vietnam's National Day.

He asked to be cremated and his ashes divided between the three main regions of Vietnam, but, in true Communist style, he was embalmed and is displayed in the imposing mausoleum bearing his name in Hanoi (see p54). His frail, bearded figure lying in a glass box is a strangely moving sight, with thousands of visitors queuing up daily to pay their respects.

charismatic figure, wearing a Chinese-style tunic and rubber-tyre sandals, carrying a small rattan trunk and his beloved typewriter. Along with other idealistic anti-colonialists, such as Vo Nguyen Giap, he founded the Viet Minh or League for the Independence of Vietnam, a united front that trained a band of patriotic guerrillas. He was arrested in 1942 by the authorities and languished in jail for over a year, writing a collection of poetry later known as the 'Prison Diary'. When the Japanese occupation of Vietnam ended at the end of World War II, the Viet Minh seized

Walk: Around the French Quarter

This walk takes you round Dong Khoi and Nguyen Hue, the two most important streets in District One. It is best undertaken in the late afternoon or early evening, when the heat of the city is less intense. This is a pleasant, languid walk, aimed at enjoying the atmosphere of 'Saigon' rather than ticking off sights in the city.

Allow 1¹/₂ hours, excluding stops for dinner or drinks.

Start at Lam Son Square, once the most elegant in the city.

1 Continental Hotel

If you haven't done so already, it is worth popping into the Continental Hotel (*see p121*) to look around.

Walk through the front doors and down the short corridor straight ahead, keeping the staircase on your right. Through the doors is the central courtyard, where you can take a drink and savour the colonial atmosphere. To take the experience to the limit, buy a

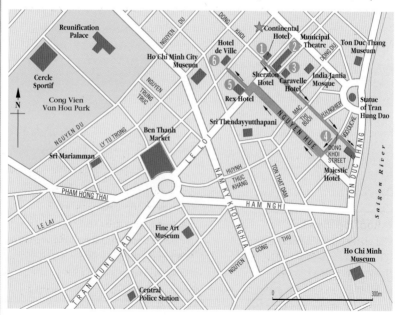

copy of Graham Greene's novel *The Quiet American* from one of the many hawkers selling photocopied books, and skim through to find descriptions of the hotel.

Coming out of the hotel, you will see the theatre in front of you, dwarfed by the elegant Caravelle Hotel behind it.

2 Municipal Theatre

The Municipal Theatre (*see p121*) stands in the middle of Lam Son Square. Whether due to good design, planning or sheer accident, the theatre is blessed with lots of space around it, which contributes to the feeling of elegance. The building has been lovingly restored and looks stunning in the late afternoon light. Lovers park their motorbikes at the bottom of the steps and sit to gaze down Le Loi street, feeling the rhythm of the city around it. All around the theatre are trendy bars and restaurants, filled with expats enjoying the cool evening air.

Walking down the theatre steps, you will see the traffic flowing down Dong Khoi street on your left. If you feel like a relaxing drink, head either to the Caravelle Hotel here or the Sheraton Hotel, a couple of hundred metres down Dong Khoi street on your left.

3 Rooftop views

The views from the rooftop bars at either the Caravelle Hotel or the Sheraton Hotel are stunning.

Keep on going southeast along Dong Khoi towards the river.

4 Dong Khoi

All along this street (*see p120*) are fancy restaurants, both Western and Vietnamese. On your right is the Underground Bar, a favourite expat watering hole themed on the London Underground. At the bottom of Dong Khoi are some beautiful shops selling furniture and home furnishings, as well as the historic Majestic Hotel.

Retrace your footsteps back up Dong Khoi, and look out for the elegant alley of Nguyen Thiep on your left. Walk down this alley, and turn right onto Nguyen Hue, heading north.

5 Rex Hotel

If you feel the need to rest your feet, a pit stop at this grand hotel (*see p122*) is just the thing. The garden terrace bar is open to the balmy evening, as well as providing some exceptional views of District One.

Coming out of the hotel, you will see the beautifully lit Hotel de Ville on your left.

6 Hotel de Ville

This stunning building (*see p122*) is the perfect backdrop for the park in front, which is popular with families out for an evening stroll. As a foreigner, you will attract some friendly attention and perhaps be approached by locals wanting to practise their English. This is the perfect opportunity to mix with real Vietnamese people on an equal footing.

This park links up with the pedestrian areas towards the theatre down and to your left.

OUTSIDE DISTRICT ONE

It would be easy to visit HCM City and totally miss out the sights on the outskirts. However, there is much to interest the tourist outside District One, and certainly you would do well to pick out at least one or two sights out of the centre to include in your itinerary.

The outskirts of the centre

The area to the north of the French Quarter, along Le Duan Boulevard, has different feel from that of the city centre, more sedate and relaxed. The Jade Emperor Pagoda is definitely worth a special journey, and can easily be combined with a visit to the Botanical Gardens and the History Museum.

US Consulate

There is not much to see here at this characterless modern building, but its predecessor, the American Embassy, held many ghosts and memories. It operated between 1967 and 1975, and was left derelict when the Americans departed, a sad legacy of the US involvement in Vietnam. In 1999 it was replaced by the present structure. Perhaps its most traumatic hour came when Northern troops attacked the Embassy on 31 January 1968 as part of the Tet Offensive and occupied part of the compound, killing five US guards. Although the compound was recaptured, the effect on the US public through the widespread press coverage of the battle was catastrophic.

THE EVACUATION OF SAIGON

With the North Vietnamese army closing in on Saigon by 1975, the US planned a helicopter evacuation of remaining Western citizens. All foreigners were to gather at 13 chosen zones upon hearing the radio broadcast of Bing Crosby's 'White Christmas' and the words 'It is 112 degrees and rising'. On 29 April 1975, the signal was broadcast, and helicopters from the US Navy's Seventh Fleet started shuttling passengers to safety. In a period of 18 hours, 2,000 people were airlifted from the US Embassy roof, with thousands of Vietnamese desperately trying to get a lift too. US Ambassador Graham Martin caught the last chopper out, together with the Stars and Stripes. These chaotic scenes were broadcast on TV around the world, signalling a close to American involvement in Vietnam.

Americans realised that the war could not be won. Now, only a plaque marks the existence of the previous building on the site.

Botanical Gardens

Developed in 1864 by the French, the gardens are not as resplendent with tropical flora as they were in colonial days, but they are reasonably well tended nevertheless. The main function of the gardens, still highly popular with couples and families, has remained unchanged. The writer Norman Lewis commented that on Sunday mornings in the 1950s, the gardens would be full of 'clusters of Vietnamese beauties … gliding in decorous groups … sometimes accompanied by gallants.' There is also an amusement park and zoo, the latter being best avoided, owing to the poor conditions in which the animals are kept.

The gate is at the far northeastern end of Le Duan. Open: daily 7am–10pm. Admission charge.

Jade Emperor Pagoda

For many people, this is one of the highlights of the city, and definitely its most beautiful pagoda. The tree-lined courtyard with its grubby pond belies the beauty that lies within. What it lacks in size it makes up for in atmosphere and interest. The air is thick with clouds of incense, illuminated by shafts of light that gleam from holes cut out of the roof. The pagoda was built in 1900 by the Chinese community, with both Taoist and Buddhist deities inside. The Jade Emperor sits in the main shrine flanked by four guards known as the Big Diamonds. The Master of

Hell, Thanh Hoang, and his red horse occupy the room to the left of the altar.

73 Mai Thi Luu. Open: daily 6am–6pm. Admission free.

National History Museum

Housed is an attractive building with a pagoda roof, this museum illuminates the country's history from its origins to the end of French rule. It is fair to say that it is less than the sum of its parts. There are several highlights, such as a 1,500-year-old wooden Buddha, some exquisite Japanese ceramics, and a 19th-century mummy. If you aren't likely to see the Water Puppets in Hanoi, the Water Puppet Theatre here is the next best place.

2 Nguyen Binh Khiem. Tel: (08) 829 8146. Open: Mon–Sat 8–11am and 1.30–4pm, Sun 8.30am–4pm. Admission charge.

The main shrine at the Jade Emperor Pagoda

Walk: Around the northeast of the centre

This walk takes you along one of the most elegant boulevards in the city, Le Duan, towards the Botanical Gardens, and then on to the Jade Emperor Pagoda. It is recommended that a taxi or xe om *is taken back to the city centre at the end of the walk.*

Allow 2 hours. Start at Notre Dame Cathedral, one of the most visible landmarks in the city.

1 Notre Dame Cathedral

This imposing building (*see p121*) dominates an area of wide boulevards and smart office blocks. The park in front of the cathedral is a pleasant place to sit and enjoy the surroundings. You may well attract the attention of friendly hawkers and *xe om* drivers eager to be of service.

Walk to the back of the cathedral and turn right, walking along Le Duan Boulevard.

2 Le Duan Boulevard

In the colonial years, this was known as Norodom Boulevard, and ran all the way to the Presidential Palace (now the Reunification Palace), a serene diplomatic and residential enclave. Its current name commemorates the secretary-general of the Worker's Party from 1959.

A series of new edifices breaks up the colonial charm. Look out on your left for the US Consulate, a nondescript building.

3 US Consulate

This building (*see p128*) replaced the former American Embassy, rich with infamous

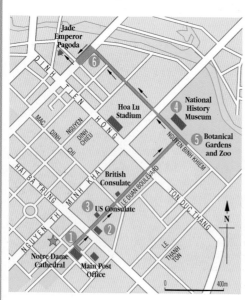

history from the American War. It is on this site that the Communists launched a daring attack on the Embassy, the heart of US power in Vietnam, in 1968. Seven years later, a helicopter evacuation from the roof marked an ignominious end to the US presence in the country. It is understandable that the Americans chose to rebuild something unassuming on the site.

Continue walking along Le Duan until you see the pagoda-style roof slightly to the left of the avenue's end.

4 National History Museum

This museum (*see p129*) has some stunning pieces, which are well worth seeking out rather than attempting to see all the exhibits. Dioramas illustrating some of the key moments in Vietnam's history help to liven up the sometimes mundane trawl through the country's past.

Just outside of the museum, you will see the gate of the Botanical Gardens.

5 Botanical Gardens

Strolling around these gardens (*see p128*) offers a pleasant respite from the fumes and noise of the city. It's an ideal location for people-watching and enjoying the gardens, rather than entering the zoo, which is a depressing experience.

Coming back out of the gardens, turn right onto Nguyen Binh Khiem and walk northwards for ten minutes until the end of the road. At the T-junction, turn left onto the broad avenue of Dien Bien Phu, and look out on your right for a spectacular pagoda on Mai Thi Luu.

6 Jade Emperor Pagoda

Perhaps the most captivating pagoda in the city; its perfumed, candle-lit rooms, the darkness lit up by shafts of light from gaps in the ceiling, lend it a magical air (*see p129*).

Outside of the pagoda on Dien Bien Phu again, you are sure to find taxis and xe oms to whisk you back to the centre of town.

The National History Museum, HCM City

Cholon

Visiting Cholon (Chinatown) is an experience in itself. It is very much like HCM City, only more so. Although not aesthetically pleasing or relaxing, Chinatown is so full of colour, energy and economic activity that it's worth half a day's excursion to sample it.

When the area was founded by the Chinese in the 17th century, it was 5km (3 miles) away from Saigon, linked by a single road, the long Tran Hung Dao. The war years in the 20th century saw a flood of refugees into the district and it eventually joined with the city centre to become one. The area became infamous for its opium dens, known then as 'fumeries', patronised by wealthy Asians and expats, including Graham Greene. The vices on offer were controlled for many years by the Binh Xuyen gang, and it was beyond

CHINESE LOAN SYSTEMS

The Hoa, or ethnic Chinese, have a traditional system of loans and credit. Informal groups of private borrowers meet in someone's house to agree loans, usually over food, washed down by alcohol. Winners in the bidding process offer the highest rate of interest to repay the loan on offer, an amount contributed to by everyone in the group. There is no written proof of this agreement, it is merely verbal. Some wealthy contributors have several agreements or 'tontines' going at the same time. This highly unorthodox credit system has operated successfully for centuries.

reach of French and then American law enforcement. The area now boasts a population of around half a million, with an estimated 40 per cent of the area's operations in the 'grey' market, beyond government control.

The French writer Didier Lauras described Cholon as 'a Chinese enclave

Religious paraphernalia in Cholon, Ho Chi Minh City

on Vietnamese soil, an ever-present reminder of the country's great neighbour. It works faster, sells cheaper, and remains utterly unfathomable.' Its importance to the city's economy is unchanged today, with economic activity verging on the manic. Although it seems chaotic, it is highly organised, along the lines of a merchant's guild from medieval days. Groups are formed from different areas in China, each controlling a different economic sector; for example, Fukien people specialise in catering, Canton people in retailing. They operate as congregations of powerful self-help groups with complex informal social regulations.

Binh Tay Market

This striking yellow-coloured, multi-tiered building at first glance seems to be a temple compound. In fact, it is a huge market selling everything from clothes, pottery and plastics to food produce of every description. The piles of stock everywhere, porters transporting supplies, and mass of people negotiating the narrow walkways can be overwhelming to the senses.

Just a few blocks east of the market is the pink-coloured Cha Tam Church, and the beginning of Hai Thuong Lan Ong, a street full of traditional medicine shops. Sliced roots and raw herbs from ginseng to dried bark spill out onto the pavement to dry, and the air is filled with a myriad aromas. Without too much looking you will come across medicines based on

endangered species, such as shark's teeth, tortoise shells and tiger's testicles. All these are advertised using none-too-subtle stuffed animals.

Phuoc An Hoi Quan Temple

One of the most beautiful temples in Cholon is this early 20th-century building, standing on the former site of a communal house. An exquisite wood carving depicts a king being entertained by minstrels and jesters, while the sanctuary contains the red-faced Quan Cong, a famous general. Many visitors rave about the atmospheric side chambers, full of rosewood furniture, mounted stag heads and photographs. *184 Hung Vuong, on the corner of Thuan Kieu. Open: daily 7am–5pm. Admission free.*

Entrance to Binh Tay Market

Thien Hau Temple, Cholon

Thien Hau Temple

The other important temple in Cholon is this one, dedicated to the Goddess of the Sea, which many new arrivals from China would have come to express gratitude to, for a safe passage across the South China Sea. Now, many local women come here to make offerings to the Goddesses of Fertility, Mothers and Newborn Babies. The highlight of the temple is undoubtedly the ceramic figurines, inspired by the legend of the Three Kingdoms, which cram the roof.

710 Nguyen Trai. Open: daily 6am–5.30pm. Admission free.

North of Cholon

The two famous pagodas just north of Cholon have a different style and ambience to those in the city centre. They are more authentic, characterful

and, arguably, more beautiful. Although they seem quite a way out of the city centre, they are only 15 or 20 minutes away on the back of a *xe om* or by taxi, and well worth the journey. Many *xe om* or taxi drivers will negotiate a reasonable half-day rate with you if you tell them your requirements.

Giac Vien Pagoda

Situated on the edge of the countryside, on a dirt track lined by shanty houses, this 18th-century pagoda has an atmosphere of intense calm. Emperor Gia Long was said to be a regular visitor. The darkness is punctuated with the squeak of bats who live in the smoky rafters. The main sanctuary contains an array of deities and a golden Buddha sitting on a lotus flower. Hai Tinh Giac Viena, the founder of the pagoda, is displayed in statue form holding a fly-swat, along with two successors. There are around 20 hospitable monks who live in the compound. Don't be surprised if they offer you a seat and a cup of tea.

Head southwest along Lac Long Quan and take a right turn at No 247, then turn left then right. Most taxi and xe om drivers know how to get there. Open: daily. Admission free.

Giac Lam Pagoda

This sprawling compound is one of the oldest pagodas in the city, and is highly popular owing to its disorganised charm. Ninety-eight hardwood pillars, terracotta floor tiles, antique tables, chandeliers and innumerable gold statues fill the spaces in this spacious building. To the sides are funerary tablets and photos of beloved ancestors. Chuan De, a many-armed goddess, stands in the middle of the chamber. The courtyard contains an attractive pond, with a model mountain in the centre, and a porcelain-decorated roof. Monks patiently smile at you as you wander round the clutter, taking in the serene atmosphere of the place. The classroom at the back of the complex contains painted panels depicting the ten Buddhist hells, in gruesome detail. At the front gate is a new tower that you can climb to admire the views from each of the six levels.

118 Lac Long Quan. Open: daily. Admission free.

Ancestor tablets and pictures at Giac Vien Pagoda

HO CHI MINH CITY ENVIRONS AND EXCURSIONS

While Hanoi is set much more in the countryside, with lots of places to visit around it, Ho Chi Minh City's position as the country's economic powerhouse, fuelled partly by its proximity to the rice bowl of Vietnam, the Mekong Delta, means that is has less to see around it. The delta, however, has much to offer the visitor. Out of the many trips that can be taken from Ho Chi Minh City, the following are the most popular.

Cu Chi Tunnels

A tour to this site is the most popular day-trip out of the city, and understandably so. It is a challenging

A trap used by the Viet Cong, Cu Chi Tunnels

Cu Chi Tunnels

experience to crawl through tunnels used by the villagers around Cu Chi district to shelter from US bombing. The fact that some of the tunnels have been specially widened for tourist-sized bodies does not detract from the claustrophobia that permeates the damp passageways.

The first tunnels in the area were built in 1948 by the Viet Minh in the war against the French, but the network was enlarged dramatically from 1960 onwards, when the Americans tried desperately to control the 'strategic zone' around Saigon. Carpet-bombing, deforestation and the relocation of villages were used to try to disrupt Viet Cong supply routes and military bases. The tunnels reached a total length of

A tank destroyed by the Viet Cong, Cu Chi Tunnels

250km (155 miles), with huge amounts of clay soil dug up and disposed of in rivers under the cover of darkness. The American military tried to break up the network by entering the tunnels using sniffer dogs and soldiers nicknamed 'tunnel rats', but suffered horrendous casualties due to the ingenuity and deadliness of the booby traps used to protect the key points of the network.

Out of the two sites where the tunnels can be seen, Ben Dinh and Ben Duoc, the former is more commonly visited by tour groups. Presentations of the tunnels and a short movie shown at the start of tours are only marginally informative, because of the sheer weight of tourist numbers, who are shepherded chaotically around the complex.

It's the tunnels themselves and the exhibits around them that are the most informative and thought-provoking. Jungle booby traps, models of mines and reconstructed underground rooms all illustrate the desperate living conditions and savage guerrilla warfare tactics that were used in these tragic years. For those wanting to live the experience more deeply, there is a firing range where you can shoot real ammunition from weapons such as the AK47 used by the Viet Cong.

45km (28 miles) northwest of HCM City, reached by taking Highway 22 to the village of Cu Chi and beyond. Tel: (08) 794 6442. Open: daily 7am–5pm. Admission charge.

The Cao Dai Pagoda

Cao Dai Pagoda

This massive cathedral is not to everyone's taste, but it certainly is eye-catching and a popular excursion out of the city. It is the headquarters of the Cao Dai religion and comprises several buildings, some administrative, some accommodation, all set in a leafy park.

The Great Temple of the Holy See of Tay Ninh, as it is sometimes called, is part pagoda, part cathedral and part Taoist place of worship. Many visitors plan their trip to attend the midday service (which is a bit of a tourist event). Worshippers dressed generally in white, but also in yellow, blue and red (signifying different religions), chant and nod occasionally, while a string band in the gallery plays religious music. Priests wear hats decorated with the Divine Eye, a highly symbolic theme that is echoed throughout the cathedral décor. Visitors occupy the gallery upstairs where they can take photos and observe the service.

The complex has been the headquarters of the Cao Dai religion since 1927, while the monastery building itself was built in 1933. Graham Greene described it as 'a Walt Disney fantasia of the East, dragons and snakes in Technicolor'.

For more information on Caodaism, *see p21*.
5km (3 miles) west of Tay Ninh, signposted to Long Hoa. Ceremonies are at 6am, noon, 6pm and midnight. Respectful attire should be worn. The use of flash is forbidden.

Water parks

When the heat and frenetic bustle of HCM City get too much, a visit to one of the water parks just outside the city is the answer.

Saigon Water Park

This is the longest-established water park around the city, with some excellent facilities that will impress both adults and kids. It has some big, sophisticated slides, as well as several pools, including a wave pool. For the less energetic, the park has a pretty stream, and a restaurant with good views. An ideal solution for cooling down, especially in the heat of the dry season.

8km (5 miles) east of HCM City, in Thu Duc District. Tel: (08) 879 0456. Open: weekdays 9am–5pm and weekends 8.30am–6.30pm. Admission charge. Buses leave from Ben Thanh bus station, the other side of the big roundabout to the indoor market.

Vietnam Water World

More modern, with more choice of facilities and bigger, but it is further out of town. Use of the tents on the camp-ground is free.

20km (12 miles) outside HCM City. Tel: (08) 897 7977. Open: Tue–Sun 8.30am–5pm. Closed: Mon. Admission charge. Buses leave from 55b Nguyen Thi Minh Khai, behind the Reunification Palace.

Shark Waterland

Located in Cholon, and therefore much more accessible. It has slides, pools and other facilities but is smaller than the others.

4km (2¹/₂ miles) west from HCM City centre. Tel: (08) 853 7867. Open: daily 10am–9pm. Admission charge. The quickest mode of transport is a taxi or the back of a xe om.

A prayer session within the Cao Dai Pagoda in Tay Ninh

The Mekong Delta

This huge area to the south of Ho Chi Minh City is a fascinating, diverse mixture of waterways, canals, paddy fields and river-bound villages that should not be missed. The vast Mekong Delta dominates the region both physically and culturally. Floating villages and markets, boats of every size and description, close-knit towns and friendly, warm people are all here to be discovered.

'The rice bowl of Vietnam', the region provides nearly 40 per cent of the country's food, not only rice but also coconuts, fruit and sugar. The name Cuu Long ('Nine Dragons') refers to the nine outlets of the huge Mekong

The Mekong Delta

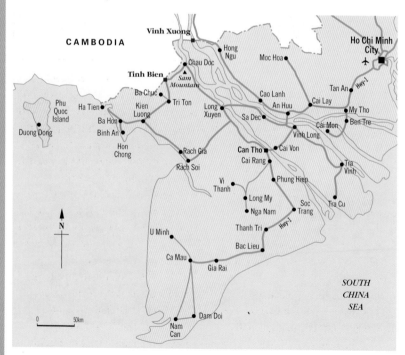

A boat delivering rambutans in the Mekong Delta

River, which travels 4,025km (2,500 miles) from its source in Tibet. Flooding has always been a problem, despite a huge network of canals aimed at channelling the water. Agriculture here only really took off when the French colonial rulers realised the potential of the rich fertile land. Until then marshland dominated the landscape, ruled by the Cambodian Khmers until the 17th century and then the Nguyen Viet lords until the mid-19th century.

Many tours here originate from HCM City, with three- or four-day trips visiting the delta's main towns and cultural attractions. In view of the seasonal flooding, the best time to visit is in the dry season (December–May). Boat tours take in the waterways of My Tho, Vinh Long and Can Tho, the latter famous for its floating market at Cai Rang. Floating houses can be visited at Chau Doc, while there are bird sanctuaries at Tam Nong near Cao Lanh. Travellers heading to Cambodia tend to take a delta tour that continues to the nearby Cambodian border rather than return to HCM City.

One destination isolated from the delta mainland is Phu Quoc Island. Often overlooked in the past, it is emerging as one of the hottest new beach destinations in Southeast Asia.

Rice

The importance of rice to the Vietnamese in both economic and cultural terms cannot be overestimated. It is not only the basis for most of their meals, but is the country's most important crop. The importance of rice is illustrated in the number of words used to describe it, in the same way that Eskimos have many words for the various conditions of 'snow'. Rice in the field is called *lua*; uncooked or raw rice is called *gao*; cooked rice is *com*. In fact, the phrase for inviting someone for a meal is *an com*, literally meaning 'let's eat rice'.

Rice is planted on 82 per cent of the total farm area of the country and accounts for more than 85 per cent of its food grain output. Vietnam became the world's second-largest rice exporter in 1997, shipping approximately 3.5 million tons.

The Vietnamese describe their country as two great rice baskets on either end of a carrying pole. In the north, the Red River Delta surrounds Hanoi to provide rice for the residents of North Vietnam. Down in the south the tremendously fertile Mekong Delta produces about 50 per cent of the country's total rice output. The people of the south refer to the rice fields as *co bay thang canh*, meaning the land is so large that the cranes can stretch their wings as they fly.

The relatively low quality of Vietnamese rice has kept export prices problematically low, but the Vietnamese government is striving to reverse this by turning the Mekong Delta into a base of high-quality rice production. Regional farmers are currently using more than 100 rice varieties.

A rice famer near Kon Tum

Working in paddy fields

The Vietnamese prefer long-grain rice in cooking to the glutinous short grain variety preferred in Northern Thailand and Japan. Rice is also used to make noodles and rice paper. Rice is cooked and pounded before being fed through a machine to make noodles, or rolled, cooked and laid out to dry in the sun on big, flat basket trays. Villages in the Mekong Delta have developed their own cottage industries making rice paper and rice-based snacks. Puffed rice is a popular treat in the Delta. It is toasted and has a crunchy, nutty flavour, very like western toffee popcorn. These snacks are marketed in Ho Chi Minh City and to tourists in the delta.

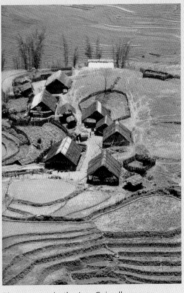

Rice terraces in the Lao Cai valley area

My Tho

My Tho is often the destination of one-day tours out of HCM City, and visited by those who do not have time to spend longer in the area. This industrious and amiable town was established in the 17th century by Chinese fleeing present-day Taiwan. Now the town is an important commercial centre where traders buy produce to sell in HCM City. It sits on the delta's northernmost branch, the Tien Gang, and is geared up for boat trips further afield.

The town itself has few sights, but the Chinese Quarter is pleasant to walk around. Vinh Trang Pagoda, set in a coconut grove 1km (^{2}/3 mile) east of the city centre, is also worth a visit. Boats are available to take you to the river islands. Chief among these is Phung (Phoenix) Island, also known as 'The Coconut Monk Island', after a local monk who founded his own sect there. There is a tacky sanctuary to him which attracts crowds of Vietnamese. Thoi Son (Unicorn Island) is the largest of the four islands off the shore of My Tho, and is a popular stopoff for tour groups to sample the local exotic fruit, including sapodilla and longon. The boat trip here, along the luxuriantly vegetated channels, is recommended. You will also probably pass the floating market, open at high tide only.

Vinh Long

The main reason for coming here is to savour delta life and to enjoy the stunning vistas over the fields. There is little to see in the town itself other than the rare Confucian shrine of the Van Thanh Mien Temple, 1km (^{2}/3 mile) south.

Perhaps the best area to visit is known by locals as An Binh Island, comprised of pockets of land broken up by channels and gullies. It can be accessed via a 5-minute ferry from town across the Co Chien River or via the 1.5km (1 mile) suspension bridge, built with Australian money, and a tourist attraction in its own right because of the beautiful views from it. A visit to the floating market at Cai Be is also recommended; it starts at 5am and finishes at 11am. Here you will see piles of pineapples, carrots, sweet potatoes and, of course, rice. Home stays can be arranged, and these are increasingly popular with tourists to the delta.

Around Binh Hoa Phuoc Island just nearby are canals leading to a beautiful floating market and the mangrove swamp. It is easy to be lulled into a peaceful relaxed mood, despite the constant noise of motors, by watching the different boats, big and small, and the boatmen greeting each other heartily as they ply their trade along the waterways.

Sa Dec

Timeless river scenes and colourful flower markets are what attract visitors to Sa Dec. Fans of Marguerite Duras, the French novelist, also come here, to see the setting for the film *The Lover*,

THE COCONUT MONK

Nguyen Thanh Nam was a visionary born in 1909 whose claim to fame was that he meditated for three years eating just coconuts. After studying in France, he developed a new religion, inspired by Buddhism and Christianity, called Tinh Do Cu Si. The Dao Sect, as it was known, had a community on Phung Island with 2,000 disciples. However, his sect found little favour with either the South Vietnamese government under Diem or the Communists after 1975. After several stints in jail, he died in 1990.

The majority of tourists to Sa Dec visit the town for its flowers. Qui Dong is the famous flower village, where a multitude of farms cultivate fruit trees, shrubs, ferns and flowers, grown on raised platforms. On Sundays the village is packed with tourists from HCM City. The most popular section of the village is Tu Ton Rose Gardens, growing not only roses, but also medicinal herbs, chrysanthemums, carnations and orchids, many of which are exported.

based on her book of the same title. The novelist herself grew up in the town, and her childhood home can be visited, a crumbling old colonial villa with a red-tiled roof and faded green shutters. It is now a police station, so you cannot see the interior. To get there, take the ferry from halfway down Nguyen Hue street. Near the house is Trung Vuong Primary School, which Duras attended.

THE LOVER

This famous novel by Marguerite Duras tells the story of a young French girl, her dysfunctional family, and the girl's journey into adulthood. She meets a wealthy Chinese man from Cholon, HCM City, on a Mekong Delta ferry and embarks upon a tempestuous affair with him. The melancholy narrative is told by the girl herself, now a woman. In 1992 the novel was turned into a film that caused controversy for its steamy sex scenes.

Ferry boat at Vinh Long with the bridge in the far distance

Can Tho

A thriving port and the biggest city in the delta, with nearly half a million inhabitants, Can Tho is a lively but pleasant city. There are many attractions, including the famous Cai Rang floating market, the smaller Phung Hiep market, and enough water channels to drift peacefully around the area for hours. Lying at the confluence of the Hau Giang and Can Tho rivers, the city is a major trading centre, transport hub, university town and administrative centre for the region. Ships ply to and from Hong Kong laden with prawns, fruit and rice on the outward journey and coming back with manufactured goods. The town itself is not as ugly as it first appears upon arriving. It has wide avenues, a pleasant riverside promenade and lively streets.

Can Tho's markets

The covered market in town is a jumble of sounds and smells, teeming with throngs of people from the surrounding area who buy and sell their produce here. The market is on Hai Ba Trung, a short distance from Ho Chi Minh's statue. Cai Rang Floating Market is the main draw in town. Located 7km (4 miles) out of Can Tho, it is perhaps the most popular market for tourists in the delta. Boats of every type are laden with produce, commonly displaying a sample hanging from a bamboo mast. Every imaginable product and service is available, from haircuts to coffins. A smaller market is at Phung Hiep, 30km (19 miles) south of the town. The best way to see it is to stroll through the lanes of the market, before walking to the riverside to see the multitude of boats along the water's edge. Vendors shout out to advertise their goods, selling mounds of fresh goods such as chillies, baguettes, squid, crab and paper flowers.

Chau Doc

While this is not a particularly beautiful or prosperous town, it has attractions that keep it on the tourist map: the fascinating floating villages outside the town, some outstanding views over the Hau Giang River and the fantastic panorama from the top of nearby Sam Mountain. The town's position near the border of Cambodia makes it an ideal point at which travellers can choose to veer across the border rather than return to HCM City. In fact, the area was ruled by the Cambodians for many years, and was attacked by Pol Pot's Khmer Rouge army in the late 1970s, leading to the Vietnamese invasion of Cambodia which overthrew Pol Pot.

Floating villages

Many tours organise small boats for tourists to drift in and out of the waterways, exploring the floating villages upstream. It comes as a surprise to realise that some stilt houses have such creature comforts as televisions, flower-decked balconies and even pet dogs that gambol along the narrow wooden planks joining the houses. Most families keep a small stock of live fish for their own consumption or for sale in the market.

Sam Mountain

The views from the summit of this 230m (755ft) high mountain are quite beautiful. More a large hill than a mountain, it nevertheless looks incongruous amongst the utterly flat landscape of rice paddies around it. It is known by locals as Nui Sam and is highly popular during pilgrimage season, when it becomes inundated with worshippers. The pagodas, shrines and parks dotted around the mountain, such as Tay An Pagoda, have a distinctly kitsch feel, more suitable for Vietnamese tastes than Western.
7km (4 miles) southwest of Chau Doc. The walk to the top takes around 40 minutes, starting from the Thoai Ngoc Hau Mausoleum. Alternatively, a xe om *will take you up the steep road.*

Views over the Hau Giang River

The main market is worth seeing if only for the little shopping streets that seem to teeter over the river, held back precariously by stilts on the water's edge. It is near here that several waterways meet, and an array of boats can be viewed drifting along the Hau Giang River. For some, the views are as stunning as anything else in the Mekong Delta.

Ha Tien

Some travellers describe Ha Tien as the quaintest town in the delta. Here you will find crumbling colonial buildings, mats of seafood drying in the sun, and shuttered terraces. Other draws to the town are the nearby beaches and attractive temples. Although it is a sizeable town of 100,000 people, it has an isolated, 'end-of-the-line' feel, only a few kilometres from the Cambodian border. It was founded in 1674 by a Chinese immigrant called Mac Cuu,

Life on the river near Chau Doc

who took advantage of its position on the trade route between India and China. His family continued to own the town as a quasi-fiefdom until 1867, when the French took over.

Nui Lang Hill

Mac Cuu and his relatives are buried around the sanctuary dedicated to him, just west of the town, past the street bearing his name. It is worth climbing this hill (called 'Nui Lang Hill' or 'Hill of Tombs'), as the views from the top are impressive.

Hon Chong headland

Many visitors come primarily for the beaches, calm waters and palm-fringed sands. To be fair, they are not as attractive as those on Phu Quoc Island (*see below*), and the scenery is blighted by ugly cement factories. The peninsula's principal town is Binh An, although the main accommodation can be found 2km (1¼ miles) south of the town. The best beach is Duong Beach, 1.5km (1 mile) further south, and set in an attractive cove, with two rocky islets called Hon Phu Tu (Father and Son Isle), a sanctuary for swifts.

Phu Quoc Island

This beautiful island in the Gulf of Thailand is fast becoming one of the top tourist destinations in Vietnam. It has stunning beaches and lush forests, features that are not lost on the growing number of developers flocking to the island.

Known as Kho Tral by the Cambodians, the island was part of the Khmer empire up until the 18th century. Cambodia has always contested ownership of the island, which is just 15km (9 miles) from its coast. At 45km (28 miles) long from north to south, it is Vietnam's largest offshore island. Its geographical isolation has had a big influence on its history. In the 1770s, Prince Nguyen Anh hid here when fleeing the Tay Son uprising, later to reclaim the throne with French assistance.

Today, 85,000 people live on the island. Facilities are limited; there are few tarmac roads, electricity is scarce in some areas, and services such as internet connections are few and far between. This is all set to change, when investment by property developers and the expansion of the airport starts to take effect. Until then, the island makes its living mainly from exports of black pepper and *nuoc-mam* (fish sauce), for which it is famous.

West coast

The west coast of the island is where most of the action takes place. The airport is situated very near the main town of Duong Dong, while the best beaches are just south, in a spectacular expanse of white sand called Bai Truong ('Long Beach'). Bai Truong is where most of the resort hotels and guesthouses line up. The beach stretches for more than 30km (19 miles) to the southern tip of the island. North of

Duong Dong is Long Lang beach, with beautiful bays and secluded sands. This stretch is less developed and an ideal spot to 'get away from it all'. The stretch of sand leading to the northwestern tip of the island was until recently occupied by the army and therefore out of bounds. Now however, this stunning area, known as Bai Dai, has been earmarked for major resort development.

At the tip of the island is Ganh Dau, a pretty fishing village set in a delightful bay. There are two islands at either end of the west coast, famous for their diving and snorkelling. The An Thoi Islands to the south contain spectacular reefs, possibly the best dive site in Vietnam. Turtle Island to the north is less visited, being near Cambodia.

The rest of the island

The interior and east coast of the island are underdeveloped, but they do have their attractions, although to a much lesser degree than the western part.

The magnificent virgin forest which covers 70 per cent of the interior of the island can be explored on foot with a guide. The hiking is excellent, although there are no marked paths, and you are likely to be covered with a film of red dust from the rough tracks that form the majority of the roads. During the dry season (November to March) visit the cleansing springs in the centre of the island. Called Suoi Da Ban and Suoi Chanh (Source of the Chanh), these are delightful shady springs popular with young locals.

The beaches on the east coast are quiet and vary in attractiveness. The most impressive is Bai Sao (Star Beach), towards the bottom of the east coast, popular with locals, especially at the weekends, with dazzling white sands and pale blue water. Here you can find small restaurants specialising in fresh seafood. Further south, almost at the tip of the island, is Bai Khem (Ice Cream Island), which is partly used as a military base. Although it has beautiful sand, it has a tendency to attract rubbish washed up by the tide.

A beautiful sandy beach on Phu Quoc Island

Getting away from it all

Sightseeing in Vietnam can be tiring, especially for those who try to see the whole country in just a week or two. Therefore it is a good idea to incorporate some downtime in your schedule for just relaxing or indulging in some restful pastimes. The good news is that there is a lot of choice available.

Beaches, water sports and boating

Perhaps the best beaches can be found at Phu Quoc Island. The beaches at Vung Tau, just north of the Mekong Delta, are more accessible from Ho Chi Minh City, although they are not so clean. Nha Trang has a wide expanse of beach and extensive facilities, while Mui Ne offers more seclusion and privacy. For more details on watersports, *see p161*. Those who require less strenuous activity can charter a boat for a leisurely sea or river cruise. The best places in the Mekong Delta for this are My Tho, Vinh Long, Can Tho and Chau Doc. Nha Trang offers a lot of choice for those who want to hire a boat. Hoi An is also recommended, with boats sailing down the Perfume River to nearby Hué and its Royal Mausoleums.

Enjoying nature

Although Vietnam has only recently started to build its ecotourist credentials, there is a wide range of options for nature-lovers.

Hiking, riding and cycling

Many hikers tend to head for Sapa in the north of the country, with a range of walks and more strenuous climbs. Less frequented but also recommended is the Ciu Mom Ray Nature Reserve near Kon Tum, a rugged, mountainous region with virgin forest and opportunities to view rare monkeys. Mai Chau, conveniently near to Hanoi, is also popular with walkers. There is good hiking, horse riding and cycling in the countryside around Dalat.

Other ecotourist options

Numerous national parks are being developed across the country with ecotourism in mind.

Cuc Phuong National Park, between Nam Dinh and Thanh Hoa in the north, is famous for its primate rescue centre, but it also offers excellent facilities to enjoy the rainforest, bird and mammal species and springtime butterfly displays. Visitors can also stay overnight in the park.

Cat Ba, an island in Halong Bay, is popular for walking. Built on limestone, the island supports a range of habitats, including marine reserves and a host of medicinal plants.

Bach Ma near Hué is home to a rich variety of plants and animals, with user-friendly trails for bird-watching and nature-lovers. It has good facilities, including marked trails, campsites and guesthouses.

Yok Don is Vietnam's largest wildlife preserve. It is famous for elephant trekking, with a variety of safaris and tours available.

Cat Thien, just southwest of Dalat, has excellent bird-watching and a host of rare animals, including the Javan rhinoceros. It is the largest lowland tropical rainforest in south Vietnam. Although it is relatively close to HCM City, its tourist facilities are limited.

The **Tam Nong Bird Sanctuary** should be mentioned. About 45km (28 miles) northwest of Cao Lanh in the Mekong Delta, this park was set up primarily to protect the Sarus cranes and other rare birds.

Swimming in the city

Swimming is an excellent way to cool down to escape the heat of the city. Cong Vien Van Hoa Park in Ho Chi Minh City has a large swimming pool, while some big hotels in the city, such as the Majestic, also have pools which are open to non-guests for a fee. Among the hotel pools that are worth visiting in Hanoi are the Army Hotel with its refreshing salt-water pool, the Hilton Hanoi Opera, the Melia and the Nikko. Also worth mentioning are the water parks outside of Ho Chi Minh City. *See pp138–9 for full details.*

Parasailing near Nha Trang

Shopping

Shopping is a delight in Vietnam, assuming that you are comfortable with the process of bargaining. There is a rich variety of souvenirs, clothes, handicrafts, and household items made from lacquerware or wood.

What to buy

Antiques

This is a bit of a minefield, for many items are just reproductions of originals. Original items are subject to the export restrictions that apply on all items of 'cultural or historical significance', especially those over 50 years old. It is best to buy from a reputable shop, which can arrange the paperwork for you. Alternatively, excellent reproductions of antiques are available, but make sure that this is stated on the invoice.

Books

Any of the famous books on Vietnam, from war novels to historical accounts, are available on the street as photocopies, at very cheap prices. It is best to check the quality of the print and pagination first, as some copies are illegible or have pages missing!

More reliable are bona-fide bookshops with good-quality books available in English.

Clothing

The typical souvenir that most tourists go for is the obligatory conical hat (*non la*), with Hué versions including poetry inlaid into the brim ('poem hats'). Also popular are the green pith helmets, with the red star at the front, worn by the Northern Vietnamese army during the American War.

Clothing is very cheap too, with many shops specialising in silk garments, especially *ao dai* traditional

BARGAINING

It is important that you do compare prices in a couple of shops before deciding to buy. Once you know a reasonable price for something and have worked out your maximum price, then you will be in a good position to negotiate. Remember to remain cheerful and humorous always when haggling, and be prepared to start to walk out of the shop to get that final discount. Vietnam in general offers excellent bargains for the tourist, so don't try to grind the poor seller into the ground. A matter of a few cents here and there means more to the Vietnamese than to comparatively rich foreigners.

costumes with baggy silk trousers worn under a knee-length silk tunic. Tailoring is very cheap in Vietnam – Hoi An is the most popular town for this. Many tourists here indulge in a shopping frenzy, snapping up work suits, shirts, dresses, trousers and even shoes that can be copied within a day from Western mail-order catalogues or photos. Silk handbags with beautiful embroidery are also popular and very cheap, with prices in Hoi An lower than elsewhere. Vietnamese silk is not as high in quality as Thai silk, but prices are lower. Embroidered cotton is also a good buy, for example pillow cases, sheets and tablecloths.

Ethnic handicrafts

The markets around Sapa, Bac Ha and other ethnic minority regions are full of goods produced by local ethnic groups. Basketwork, mats and bags are available, while colourful fabrics worn by the minority groups are often fashioned into attractive shoulder bags, purses or hats. Ethnic handicrafts can also be found in the big cities, at a higher price.

Handicrafts

There is a huge range of articles that you can buy from a variety of materials: bronze, brass, ceramic, mother-of-pearl, jade, bamboo and wood. Tea sets including tray, cups and teapots are popular purchases, as are wooden bowls, chopstick sets and wooden carved statues. Because labour is so cheap, the value for money for exquisitely crafted items is exceptional.

Lacquerware

Among the most beautiful types of handicraft, *son mai* is made by applying successive layers of resin to wooden items and polishing it to a sheen. Chopsticks, boxes, vases, trays and photo albums are among the items that look stunning in lacquerware.

Paintings

There are a large number of art galleries of every description setting up in the tourist areas of the large towns, some specialising in Vietnamese traditional scenes, and others reproducing famous works of Western art. The quality is often very high, with prices much lower than can be found in the West. For the more up-market variety, it is best to buy from a reputable gallery to ensure that the

Vietnamese silk is a popular souvenir

work is original rather than a copy. Silk paintings are also a popular souvenir.

War memorabilia

There are a lot of trinkets, army surplus gear and dog tags that are said to be originals from the American War, but most are likely to be well-made fakes. Zippo lighters are especially popular, as are uniforms.

Where to shop

The best towns to shop in are Hanoi, Hoi An and Ho Chi Minh City, where the choice and prices are the best. Markets are slightly cheaper than shops, although the quality may not be so consistently high. Shops in the colonial parts of town, popular with foreigners, are going to be more expensive than shops in the less up-market parts of town or backpacker districts.

HANOI

Hanoi is generally thought to offer the best value and quality in Vietnam for crafts, silk and souvenirs. Of particular quality are sandalwood, embroidery, lacquerware and stone carvings. The best areas are the south of the Old Quarter, particularly Hang Gai, and the smart streets around St Joseph's Cathedral.

Art Vietnam – four floors of exhibitions from contemporary artists. *30 Hang Than. Tel: (04) 927 2349.*

Khai Silk – the town's most famous silk shops with several branches. *121 Nguyen Thai Hoc and 96 Hang Gai. Tel: (04) 747 0583.*

La Hang – Hanoi's best-known tailor. *55 Tran Nhan Tong. Tel: (04) 943 3225.*

Lan Handicrafts – a non-profit shop with quilts and other fabrics made by disadvantaged young people. *38 Nha Chung.*

Nguyen Freres – a chain of shops with superb interiors and beautiful furniture. *3 Phan Chu Trinh. Tel: (04) 933 1699.*

Tay My – three floors with a huge range of embroidery, silks and fabrics. *66 Hang Gai. Tel: (04) 825 1579.*

HOI AN

Hoi An is the place for tailoring, as well as handbags and hand-made shoes. The old town, particularly along Tran Phu, Nguyen Thai Hoc and Le Loi, is full of shops and art galleries. Those west of the Japanese Bridge are also worth looking at. There are many shops that can make shoes, near the bridge on Hoang Dieu.

Bi Bi Silk – one of the best-known tailors in town. *13 Phan Chu Trinh.*

Hoi An Handicraft Workshop – displays local crafts including embroidery, woodcarving and pottery. *9 Nguyen Thai Hoc. Tel: (0510) 910216.*

House of Traditional Handicrafts – traditional methods of craft-making can be seen, with a good range of products on sale. *41 Le Loi. Tel: (0510) 862164.*

Yaly – an up-market tailors of excellent quality. *47 Nguyen Thai Hoc. Tel: (0510) 910474.*

HO CHI MINH CITY

A large range of shopping choices is available in this city, depending on what you want and your budget. Ben Thanh market is cheapest, but the shops around Le Loi and the back of Ben Thanh market are also recommended, and sell high-quality handbags and embroidery. Dong Khoi street offers boutiques and upmarket souvenirs shops, while there are also lots of shops around Nguyen Hué and Mac Thi Buoi. The backpacker area, particularly De Tham and Pham Ngu Lao, has good-value shops, selling souvenirs, (pirated) CDs and photocopied books.

Ben Thanh market offers the lowest prices on most things, including clothes, souvenirs and handbags. There is a big selection of cheap eateries further inside too. Watch your wallet and handbag carefully. Some tourists find the crowds and full-on selling techniques off-putting, but it is well worth persevering.

Junction of Tran Hung Dao, Le Loi and Ham Nghi.

A M Lacquerware – a good range of lacquerware, bamboo and stone products at low prices. *185 Pham Ngu Lao. Tel: (08) 836 8651.*

Authentique Interiors – spacious shop with beautiful wall-hangings, textiles, homeware, clothes and other gifts. Take your credit card! *6 Dong Khoi. Tel: (08) 822 1333.*

Diamond Plaza – big shopping mall with department store and supermarket among other facilities. *34 Le Duan. Tel: (08) 822 5500.*

Saigon Centre – souvenir shops, boutiques and small department stores in a convenient location. *65 Le Loi. Tel: (08) 823 2505.*

Saigon Square – Ground-level shopping arcade with souvenir shops. *Corner of Hai Ba Trung and Nguyen Du.*

Sapa – Attractive garments and artefacts from ethnic minority groups. *222 De Tham and 64 Dong Du. Tel: (08) 827 7707.*

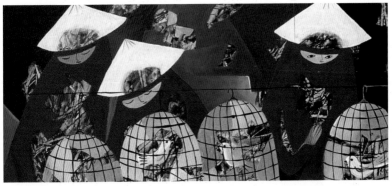
Paintings can be bought in many places, including Hanoi, Hoi An and HCM City

Entertainment

There are some entertainment options for foreigners, more so in the big cities such as Ho Chi Minh and Hanoi than in smaller towns, with events such as concerts and shows, bars with live music, and the cinema. For the Vietnamese, family life is such an integral part of their day that most evenings are spent together, often over dinner, or with friends in someone's house. Even the young tend to gather together in the streets, sitting on plastic chairs at pavement eateries, drinking cheap draught beer or soda. Alternatively they are seen on weekend nights cruising around town on their motorbikes, seeing and being seen by their peers.

However, there is a growing nightlife scene, especially in the cities, which offers some scope for tourists. For details of what's on, it is worth checking out the monthly listings in *The Guide* or weekly *Time Out* supplements. Ho Chi Minh City is much more buzzing than Hanoi, which is pretty sleepy for a capital city. For details of nightclubs, *see* 'Where to drink', *pp166–7*.

Cinema

Most towns have at least one cinema (*rap*). However, most show Vietnamese films or Western action films that are dubbed into Vietnamese. These are entertaining in themselves, though in many, the dubbing is done by one voice for all the characters, something that must be heard to be believed! Don't necessarily expect air-conditioning and surround-sound, either.

HANOI
Fansland Cinema – shows Western films. *84 Pho Ly Thuong Kiet. Tel: (04) 825 7484.*
National Movie Centre – the newest venue to catch foreign films. *87 Pho Lang Ha. Tel: (04) 514 1114.*

HO CHI MINH CITY
Rap Dong Khoi – cinema very near the Municipal Theatre. *163 Dong Khoi.*

Concerts and shows

There are organised concerts and shows in the major cities, although these are generally not well publicised. So-called 'traditional music' shows often have a liberal sprinkling of pop acts within the cabaret-style format. Traditional cultural shows are organised by the Vietnam Arts Resource and Info Centre. *Tel: (04) 511 6302. E-mail: mociford@hn.vnn.vn*

Musicians perform in the Temple of Literature, Hanoi

HANOI

Hong Ha Theatre – gives performances of Cheo, the Vietnamese equivalent of Chinese opera. *51 Duong Thanh. Tel: (04) 837 0046.*

Jazz Club (Cau Lac Bo) – nightly music shows with local and international jazz artists. *31–33 Pho Luong Van Can. Tel: (04) 828 7890.*

Opera House – Periodic performances are hosted at this magnificently restored venue. *Pho Trang Tien. Tel: (04) 933 0113.*

Thang Long Water Puppet Theatre – home to the famous Thang Long Water Puppet Troupe, who give several performances daily of *mua roi nuoc. 57 Dinh Tien Hoang. Tel: (04) 824 9494.*

HO CHI MINH CITY

Binh Quoi Village – the only real tourist-oriented venue in the city, with regular programmes of folk music and traditional dancing. *1147 Xo Viet Nghe Tinh. Tel: (08) 899 1831 or contact Saigontourist (08) 829 8914.*

Conservatory of Music – regular performances of Western and traditional Vietnamese classical music.

112 Nguyen Du, near the Reunification Palace. Tel: (08) 822 5841.

Hoa Binh Theatre – hosts performances of theatre, modern and traditional Vietnamese music, and fashion shows. *Nhat Hat Hoa Binh, District 10. Tel: (08) 865 5199.*

Municipal Theatre – periodic concerts and shows are performed here. Look out for the banners outside for what's coming up. *Lam Son Square, Dong Khoi. Tel: (08) 829 9976.*

Karaoke

Karaoke bars are recommended for the experience rather than enjoyment. Karaoke is highly popular in Vietnam, and the enthusiasm is matched by the truly awful quality of the singing. Some karaoke bars have top-notch audio and video systems, which blare out at full volume.

Watch out for *karaoke om* bars, where young women 'hold' the microphone while you sing. They are notorious for hefty hidden charges. If you do decide to stay, agree all the charges in advance.

Children

There are a lot of sights of interest and activities suitable for children, and you will be treated very well because of them, as the Vietnamese love children. However, fair-haired kids attract more attention than most and some families find this intrusive after a while. You may also have to plan your transport carefully, as road journeys are long and sometimes arduous. Hygiene is another issue that is especially relevant for children.

Health

Vietnam is not the most sanitary country, so children may be affected more than adults by bacteria and spicy foods. It is best to avoid fresh fruit juices, ice and spicy foods. It is important to drink lots of water, especially if children do get upset stomachs. Health-care facilities are fairly good in the big towns, but very basic outside. Ensure that your travel insurance includes full medical evacuation, just in case transport is needed urgently. Useful resources include the website *www.familytraveltimes.com* and various books, including Maureen Wheeler's *Travel with Children* (Lonely Planet).

Travelling

Plan your schedule carefully to avoid long road journeys. Trains are better for children as there is more scope to move around. Domestic flights are a relatively cheap and practical option wherever possible, and there are many internal flights linking most major towns. Domestic flights and bus tickets are often half-price for children. Most hotels have rooms suitable for families.

Activities

There is a range of activities in both cities and countryside for children. Zoos and parks are well recommended in cities, while nature reserves and beaches are ideal for children to enjoy the open spaces.

HANOI

Water Puppet Theatre – home to the famous Thang Long Water Puppet Troupe, who give several performances daily of *mua roi nuoc* (*see p45*). *57 Dinh Tien Hoang. Tel: (04) 824 9494.*
Central Circus – circus performances in a huge tent, with several shows weekly. *Near the northern entrance to Lenin Park (Cong Vien Le Nin), south of the city centre.*

HO CHI MINH CITY

Saigon Water Park – the city's longest-established water park (*see p139*), with excellent facilities. *8km (5 miles) east of HCM City, in Thu Duc District. Tel: (08) 8790 456.*

Botanical Gardens – well-kept gardens, with a children's amusement park and zoo (*see p128*). *The entrance is at the far northeastern end of Le Duan.*

Ho Ky Hoa Park – children's amusement park, with paddleboats, arcades and rides. *Behind the Quoc Tu Pagoda in District 10.*

Nature reserves

Cuc Phuong Cuc National Park – Famous for its primate rescue centre, but it also offers excellent facilities (*see p151*). *Between Nam Dinh and Thanh Hoa in north Vietnam. Park HQ Tel: (03) 848 006.*

Bach Ma National Park – home to a rich variety of plants and animals, with user-friendly trails for bird-watching and nature-lovers (*see p96*). *Just inland from Hué, in central Vietnam. Tel: (054) 871 330.*

Beaches

Phu Quoc Island – possibly the best beaches in Vietnam and an unspoiled atmosphere. Good opportunities for snorkelling and fishing trips. Just off the south coast of Vietnam (*see p148*).

Nha Trang – expansive beaches and excellent facilities, including private beaches owned by restaurants. Near the southeast corner of the country (*see p115*).

Mui Ne – lots of up-market resorts offering good facilities including water sports, and small secluded beaches. Just east of Phan Thiet in southern Vietnam (*see p117*).

This pavilion at Thay Pagoda near Hanoi is used for water puppet performances

Sport and leisure

Vietnam's favourite spectator sport is soccer, and European league games are televised extensively. Badminton-playing is highly popular with all age groups in Vietnam. Every morning and evening, you will see families and neighbours setting up badminton nets in local parks for a quick game before and after work. Basketball, volleyball and tennis rank next in popularity. For visitors, a range of activities, from trekking to water sports and swimming, is available.

SPORT
There are some opportunities for sport, mostly in the major cities. These are the main locations:

Cong Vien Van Hoa Park, Ho Chi Minh City. Offers tennis, badminton, and swimming facilities.

Vietnam Golf and Country Club, 15km (9 miles) east of HCM City. Visitors are welcome to use the golf course and other facilities, including driving range, tennis courts and swimming pool. *40–42 Nguyen Trai, Thu Duc district in Lam Vien Park. Tel: (08) 832 2084.*

King's Island Golf Resort and Country Club, 45km (28 miles) west of Hanoi. 18-hole golf course open to visitors. *Close to the base of Ba Vi Mountain. Tel: (04) 826 0342.*

Army Hotel, Hanoi. Guests can use this salt-water swimming pool for the day. *33C Pho Pham Ngu Lao. Tel: (04) 825 2896.*

Adventure activities
Vietnam has been slow to develop its potential as an outdoor adventure destination. However, the country's vast area is becoming increasingly accessible, with more specialist tour

Parasailing in Halong Bay

agencies offering a wider choice of activities.

Trekking is fairly low-key in Vietnam compared to its Asian neighbours, although more tours are being developed, especially in northern Vietnam and the Highlands. The most popular trekking area is around Sapa, followed by Mai Chau. Experienced hikers only should take the challenge of climbing Mount Fansipan near Sapa. The Highlands also offer many opportunities for outdoor activities, including Yok Don National Park, which is famous for elephant-trekking, Kon Tum and Dalat, which is developing rock climbing, canyoning and abseiling facilities. It is best to organise a tour or book arrangements for trekking or overnight stays in minority villages, and you should have a guide at all times if going off the beaten track.

Jogging

For those in Hanoi or Ho Chi Minh City, there are quite a few city parks that are ideal for jogging around, especially early in the morning. For example, Lenin Park just south of Hanoi city centre is popular with locals, while Cong Vien Van Hoa Park in Ho Chi Minh City is spacious and attractive.

For those who fancy a jog or walk in the countryside in the company of ex-pats, a 'Hash' with the Hash House Harriers is a fun option. The Hash House Harriers are an informal group of runners who organise weekend outings, with an emphasis on beer-drinking and socialising. For details of runs, it is a good idea to check out the notice boards in the expat bars. In Hanoi, the Spotted Cow pub on Hai Ba Trung usually posts details, while in Ho Chi Minh City, it is worth asking at the Caravelle Hotel, or the Underground bar on Dong Khoi.

Water sports

Vietnam is slowly building up its infrastructure to offer more facilities for water sports. With 3,000km (1,864 miles) of coastline, there is lots of potential. However, there are strong winds and even stronger undercurrents which compromise the safety of some beaches. The best places for water sports are:

Halong Bay – many tours here offer optional days of sea-kayaking, a great option in this stunning location (*see p68*).

Nha Trang – big beaches and lots of water-sports facilities, including jet-skiing, parasailing, scuba-diving and snorkelling around the outlying islands (*see p114*). Avoid Nov–Dec, the rainy season.

Non Nuoc Beach near Danang – known as 'New China Beach' – has a good reputation for windsurfing.

Mui Ne – famous for its international surfboard and kite-surfing competition each spring (*see p117*). Surfing is best Aug–Apr.

Phu Quoc Island – superb snorkelling and scuba-diving at the nearby An Thoi Islands, with fabulous coral reefs and lovely beaches (*see p148*).

Food and drink

Eating in Vietnam is one of the most enjoyable aspects of visiting the country, with a wonderfully varied cuisine, and many different dining experiences to choose from. Vietnam is not known for its alcohol, but there is enough choice for most tastes, as well as a huge range of delicious fruit juices and other beverages.

What to eat

Vietnamese food in general is lighter and more subtle than Thai or Indian, and incredibly varied. It is related to Chinese cuisine, but has its own traditions and dishes. Rather than stir-fries and sauces, Vietnamese dishes rely on herbs and seasoning, with boiled or steamed rice.

A wide range of culinary influences has been at work within Vietnam. In the south there are spices and curries, although even then chillies are not used in cooking, but instead used to make up dipping sauce. Northern cuisine is more closely related to Chinese cooking, with rice, noodles and meat or fish forming the main ingredients.

The French colonial period has left its mark on the country too, with baguettes, butter, cheese and pastries staying part of Vietnamese tastes well after *les colons* left the country.

There is some vegetarian fare, introduced through Buddhism, although many non-meat dishes are cooked using animal fat. However, there are specialist vegetarian (*an chay*) restaurants in the main towns, and some vegetarian rice shops (*tiem com chay*).

Popular dishes

Vietnamese dishes use rice as their main staple, with noodles an alternative at breakfast or as a snack. The most popular Vietnamese dishes are:

Bo Bay Mon – a popular southern dish, consisting of a platter of beef cooked in seven different styles.

Bo Luc Lac – Cubed spicy beef stir-fried with green pepper.

Cha Ca – a famous fish dish originating in Hanoi. Fresh fish is sautéed in butter at the table, and fresh dill and spring onions are added, served with rice noodles and ground peanuts.

Ga Xe Phay – Shredded chicken salad with bean sprouts, carrot, peanut and basil.

Noodle soup (*pho*, pronounced 'fur') – a light beef broth with flat rice noodles, spring onions and slivers of meat (commonly beef), flavoured with ginger, fresh herbs, lime juice and chilli sauce.

Spring rolls (variously known as *cha nem, nem ran or cha gio*) – typically Vietnamese, using combinations of minced pork, shrimp, rice vermicelli and bean sprouts.

Tom Hap Bia – Shrimps cooked in beer.

'Exotic' dishes

The Vietnamese have a reputation for eating animals that we in the West would balk at eating. They are reputed to eat 'anything with legs except a table and chairs, anything that flies except a plane'. Some of these, worth mentioning for mainly cultural interest, are:

Dog (*thit cay*) is a delicacy in the north, particularly in the winter, where it is said to improve body heat. Sandy-haired dogs are considered the tastiest.

Duck eggs (*trung vit lon*) – a dish only for those with cast-iron stomachs, consisting of duck eggs boiled only five days before hatching – bill, webbed feet, feathers and all.

Snake (*thit con ran*) – supposed to improve male virility. Dining on snake is surrounded by a ritual which entails the guest of honour swallowing the snake's still-beating heart.

Desserts

Turning swiftly to desserts, Vietnam is not strong on them, other than sickly candied fruits and green-coloured *banh com*, made with green-bean paste and glutinous rice. However, the range of fresh fruits is fantastic, with papaya, mango, longan, coconut and pineapple being commonly available. Specialities include dragon fruit from Nha Trang and strawberries from Dalat.

What to drink

Vietnam's national drink is green tea, which is brought out to accompany every social gathering, business or family meal and after meals. Tea drinking in general is part of the social ritual, and it is considered rude not to take at least a sip if it is offered to you. The French are said to have introduced

A bottle of Dalat white wine

coffee, the best of which is grown in Buon Ma Thuot. Vietnamese coffee is served very strong, often filtered at the table with a small dripper placed over the glass, and sweetened with condensed milk.

Alcoholic drinks

Rice wine is a popular alcoholic drink, although not usually to Western tastes. It is drunk particularly at festivals and official receptions. The most famous is brewed by the ethnic minorities in the northwest, drunk from a communal jar using thin bamboo straws. Local beers are on the whole pretty good, especially fresh beer, which is served containing slabs of ice in local street bars (*bia hoi*). Imported bottled beer, wine and spirits are increasingly available. Vietnamese wine is best avoided other than that produced in Dalat, which can be reasonable.

There are many local alcoholic drinks with supposed medicinal benefits, made from ingredients such as rice, strawberries, mulberries, snakes or herbs. You can't fail to notice them on display in some shops.

Water and soft drinks

Bottled water is sold everywhere very cheaply, but make sure that the seal is not broken. If you want to avoid tummy problems, it is best to avoid ice altogether (*dung bo da* means 'no ice'), and avoid fresh fruit juices that are diluted with tap water. Most tourist outlets are fairly safe, though.

Soft drinks in bottles, cans or cartons are widely available, although the local ones are very sweet. Western fizzy drinks are sold in most areas. Other options are fresh coconut juice or sugar-cane juice, which isn't as sweet as it sounds.

Where to eat

There is a wide range of eating establishments to choose from, depending on your budget, your inclination to try local dishes and your desire for the 'authentic' Vietnamese eating experience. It is easy to find travellers' cafés in the main towns, serving cheap but banal fare, and also Western-style restaurants serving good-quality Vietnamese and international dishes.

Street food

Street kitchens are the most 'authentic' and aimed mainly at locals; they serve some very tasty and fresh food. They vary from hawkers peddling their dish from shoulder poles or carts, to streetside restaurants with plastic tables and chairs. It is best to get there early, around 11.30am for lunch and by 7pm for dinner. They often display their dishes in glass cabinets. Many advertise their speciality on a signboard. The main words to look out for are:

Bun Bo – rice noodles mixed with shredded beef with fresh herbs and ground peanuts.

Bun Cha – small barbecued pork burgers served with rice noodles.

Chao or **Xhao** – hot, thick rice gruel with shredded chicken or fish, dill and an egg at the bottom.

Com (rice)

Com Binh Dan ('people's meals') – here you select from a variety of prepared dishes and pay for what you select.

Pho (noodles)

Restaurants

The star ratings are based on the price per head of a three-course meal with a soft drink.

★   Less than US$2
★★   US$2–5
★★★   US$5–10
★★★★   over US$10

HANOI

There is a huge range of eating establishments, from street kitchens to international restaurants, cafés and patisseries. Places in the Old Quarter tend to be less grand than those in the French Quarter.

Bun Bo Nam Bo ★
The town's most famous outlet for Bun Bo. Just sit on a bench with the locals.
67 Hang Dieu, Old Quarter.

Nguyen Tuan ★★
A little gem of a café at the back of a shop. Walk up past the family shrine to the rooftop terrace with great views of Hoan Kiem Lake.
11 Hang Gai.

Kangaroo Cafe ★★
Fresh, wholesome Western food in this Australian-run café, including excellent vegetarian food.
18 Bao Khanh. Tel: (04) 828 9931.

Little Hanoi 1 ★★
Cosy, dark, atmospheric restaurant in the Old Quarter serving excellent local and Western dishes.
14 Ta Hien.
Tel: (04) 926 0168.

Little Hanoi 2 ★★
More of an expat lunchtime favourite than its namesake, well positioned on a junction near Hoan Kiem Lake.
21 Hang Gai.
Tel: (04) 828 8333.

Cha Ca La Vong ★★
This faded restaurant is an institution, famous for its delicious *cha ca*, fish sautéed at the table with fresh dill.
14 Cha Ca.
Tel: (04) 825 3929.

Tamarind Café ★★★
Superbly presented and innovative vegetarian dishes, with prices to match. Home to the excellent Handspan Tours.
80 Ma May, Old Quarter.
Tel: (04) 926 0580.

Koto ★★★
Excellent deli-style restaurant staffed by charming former street kids trained under a charity programme. Very near the Temple of Literature.
61 Van Mieu.
Tel: (04) 747 0337.

Al Fresco's ★★★★
For those who need a fix of high-quality Western dishes like steak and pizza; an expat haunt.
23 Hai Ba Trung, French Quarter. Tel: (04) 826 7782.

Emperor ★★★★
The best of Hanoi's upmarket Vietnamese restaurants, within a traditional stilt house.
18b Le Thanh Tong.
Tel: (04) 826 8801.

HUÉ

Most restaurants are on the eastern, modern side of the river, where the main town is located, the

Food and drink

other side from the Citadel.

Lac Thanh Restaurant ★★
Backpacker hangout with excellent local food, owned by the friendly Mr Lac, who is deaf and mute.
6A Dinh Tien Hoang, the Citadel.
Tel: (054) 824674.

Dong Tam ★★
Best at lunchtime with a lovely garden courtyard and good-value vegetarian food.
66/7 Le Loi, east of the river. Tel: (054) 828403.

Paradise Garden ★★★
Pleasant river-front setting with high-quality food.
17 Le Loi, opposite the Hotel Saigon Morin.
Tel: (054) 832220.

Tinh Gia Vien ★★★★
Sumptuous French colonial setting with set meals based on Hué's imperial court, with artistically presented food.
20/3 Le Thanh Ton, the Citadel. Tel: (054) 522243.

HO CHI MINH CITY

The quality restaurants tend to be in the French Quarter, especially around Dong Khoi street.

Zen ★
Cheap, imaginative vegetarian food in the backpacker area, including great fruit shakes.
185/30 Pham Ngu Lao.
Tel: (08) 837 3713.

Bo Tung Xeo Restaurant ★★
An unassuming outdoor eatery specialising in cheap BBQ meats cooked at your table, mainly aimed at locals, but English is spoken.
31 Ly Tu Trong, short walk northeast of the Hotel de Ville.
Tel: (08) 825 1330.

Givral ★★★
An institution, in a prime spot facing the Continental Hotel, its Western food restaurant and adjoining patisserie catering mainly for up-market tourists and expats.
169 Dong Khoi.
Tel: (08) 829 2747.

Vietnam House ★★★
Superb Vietnamese food in a lovely colonial building.
95 Dong Khoi.
Tel: (08) 829 1623.

Ngon ★★★
Highly popular restaurant serving regional specialities in a delightful colonial building.
138 Nam Ky Khoi Nghia.
Tel: (08) 825 7179.

Mandarine ★★★★
Perhaps the best Vietnamese food in town, with live traditional music.
11A Ngo Van Nam, to the northeast of Lam Son Square.
Tel: (08) 822 9783.

Le Mekong ★★★★
An established French favourite, with superb French dishes.
57 Dong Du, just north of Dong Khoi.
Tel: (08) 829 5045.

Where to drink

Most places serve both food and drinks, but those listed below are particularly recommended for a pleasant drink or are bars which incorporate a nightclub. They are all in Hanoi or Ho Chi Minh City; other towns, apart from Hoi An, do not tend to have much going on at night.

HANOI

Hanoi is not as lively as Ho Chi Minh City at night, although there is nightlife if you know where to look.

Highway 4

Try and get a seat on the balmy, atmospheric terrace and taste the herbal liqueurs. Also serves food.

5 Hang Tre, near Hoan Kiem Lake.
Tel: (04) 926 0639.

Met Pub

A good excuse to visit the classy Sofitel Metropole Hotel. A British-style pub with buffet food and darts available.

15 Ngo Quyen.
Tel: (04) 829 2185.

New Century

The city's biggest, brashest nightclub, with good dance music and expensive drinks.

10 Trang Thi.
Tel: (04) 926 6919.

Press Club

Quintessential colonial atmosphere at this plush business venue.

59A Ly Thai To.
Tel: (04) 934 0888.

Spotted Cow

Australian bar full of ex-pats. Details of the local Hash House Harriers can be found on the noticeboard.

23C Hai Ba Trung.
Tel: (04) 824 1028.

The Wave

Hanoi's hottest nightclub, with a stylish lounge bar, DJs and occasional bands.

Sofitel Plaza, 2 Yen Phu.

HO CHI MINH CITY

Most nightclubs and good bars are in the French Quarter, some within smart hotels with spectacular views.

Apocalypse Now

A Saigon nightclub institution, it is a victim of its own popularity, with a rowdy crowd including prostitutes.

2C Thi Sach.
Tel: (08) 825 6124.

Panorama

An expensive bar but worth it for the views of the river and the French Quarter.

Level 32–33, Saigon Trade Centre, 37 Ton Duc Thang.
Tel: (08) 910 0492.

Rooftop Garden

Expensive drinks but a superb terrace setting in the Rex Hotel.

141 Nguyen Hué.
Tel: (08) 829 2185.

Saigon-Saigon Rooftop Bar

Superb views of the city with live music, on the 11th floor of the five-star Caravelle Hotel.

19 Lam Son Square.
Tel: (08) 824 3999.

Tropical Rainforest

Called Mua Rung by locals, this trendy nightclub has Amazonian rainforest décor.

5–15 Ho Huan Nghiep.
Tel: (08) 825 7783.

Vascos

A mainly expat hangout with a palm-shaded courtyard, pool table and regular film showings.

16 Cao Ba Quat.
Tel: (08) 824 3148.

Underground

An expat favourite with everything for the homesick foreigner, from Western food to a pool table.

69 Dong Khoi.
Tel: (08) 829 9079.

Hotels and accommodation

Vietnam now has a huge range of accommodation, with many new establishments springing up every year, especially in the tourist centres of Hanoi, Sapa, Hué, Hoi An, Nha Trang and Ho Chi Minh City.

In some towns, especially out of high season, discounts are available, and it is worth negotiating anyway as a matter of course. It is a good idea to look at a selection of rooms before choosing one, especially if you are sensitive to noise or sunlight. Remember, Vietnamese are early risers, and traffic usually gets noisy as early as 7am. Generally, rooms on higher floors at the back of the building (i.e. away from the street) are quieter. In some places, you do not need air-conditioning and a fan will suffice. If you choose not to stay at the hotel, you can always leave your luggage there while you look for another one.

Some budget hotels have an annoying habit of adding the government tax of 10 per cent onto the bill, so it is worth clarifying this before booking, in addition to checking whether breakfast is included. Hotel bills are normally paid for in US dollars. You will need to give the hotel your passport at some point during your stay, so that they can register you with the authorities.

Remember to take your passport if going on an overnight tour, as you may encounter problems otherwise.

When taking a bus, you are likely to be dropped off at a hotel that has a deal with the bus company. A representative will encourage you to look at the hotel, and the bus will take you to a selection of other hotels too. While this is frustrating at first, it must be admitted that the value for money and quality of the selected hotels is on the whole very good, and it saves walking around a new town looking for your own hotel.

The hotels listed below are some of the best in their respective price ranges (for a double room for one night).

★	Less than US$15
★★	US$15–30
★★★	US$30–80
★★★★	over US$80

HANOI

There is a wide choice of accommodation in Hanoi. Here are

some of the most popular in each price range.

The Sofitel Metropole ★★★★
One of Vietnam's great luxury hotels, drenched in exquisite colonial French décor (*see p53*).
15 Ngo Quyen.
Tel: (04) 826 6919;
www.sofitel.com

Hanoi Opera Hilton ★★★★
Looks dazzling from the outside, positioned beside the beautiful grand Opera House in the old French Quarter.
1 Le Thanh Tong.
Tel: (04) 933 0500;
www.hanoi.hilton.com

Dan Chu Hotel ★★★
Tastefully restored to retain its 19th-century charm, it is more affordable than other hotels in the district.
29 Trang Tien.
Tel: (04) 825 4937;
www.danchuhotel.com

Huyen Trang Hotel ★★
Elegant hotel with Chinese-style furnishings, near Hoan Kiem Lake.
36 Hang Trong.
Tel: (04) 826 8480;
huyetrang@fpt.vn

Tung Trang Hotel ★
Newish hotel with charming staff, situated away from the noise in a quaint Old Quarter alley.
13 Tam Thuong, off Hang Bong. Tel: (04) 8286267;
tungtranghotel@yahoo.com

Paradise Hotel ★
A comfortable quiet hotel, in an alley full of budget accommodation.
1 Yen Thai, off Hang Manh. Tel: (04) 928 6139;
thienthaijsc@fpt.vn

HUÉ

Most hotels are on the eastern, modern side of the river, where the main town is located, the other side from the Citadel, although there are some quiet, pleasant hotels (but few shops and restaurants) within the Citadel.

Saigon Morin ★★★★
The town's most famous hotel, with colonial charm and four-star standards.
30 Le Loi.
Tel: (054) 823526;
www.morinhotel.com.vn

Huong Giang ★★★
One of the town's top hotels, with a pool, gardens and some rooms with river views.
51 Le Loi.
Tel: (054) 822122;
www.huonggiangtourist. com

Thanh Noi ★★
Located near the Citadel, with imperial-style décor, although with a musty feel to it.
57 Dang Dung.
Tel: (054) 522478;
thanhnoi@dng.vnn.vn

Binh Minh 1 ★
A good-value option in a great location, with clean, pleasant rooms.
36 Nguyen Tri Phuong.
Tel: (054) 825526;
binhminhhue@dng.vnn.vn

HOI AN

Hotels are springing up at a frenetic pace in this fast-growing tourist town. It is worth haggling to get a good deal.

Victoria Hoi An Resort ★★★★
A classy hotel by the beach with expensive bungalows and villas available, a free shuttle bus into town, and excellent facilities.
Cua Dai Beach.
Tel: (0510) 927040;
www.victoriahotelsasia.com

Pacific Hotel ★★★★
Four-star standards with friendly staff and a delightful garden with pool, just out of town on the way to the beach.
167 Cua Dai.
Tel: (0510) 923 777;
www.hoianpacific.com

Ha An ★★
Serene, family-run hotel set around a lovely garden, to the east of the town.
6 Phan Boi Chau.
Tel: (0510) 863126;
tohuong@fpt.vn

Dong Khanh Hotel ★
Clean, pleasant hotel popular with Sinh Café

Hotel Majestic, HCM City

buses. A few minutes' walk from the market.
42 Nguyen Duy Hieu.
Tel: (0510) 914400;
dongkhanhhotelha@
yahoo.com

HO CHI MINH CITY

Accommodation costs slightly more here than the rest of the country, but there are lots of hotels available, especially in the French Quarter, which has the more historic, business hotels, and in the backpackers' area around Pham Ngu Lao.

Caravelle ★★★★
One of the city's most prestigious hotels in the heart of the French Quarter, with dizzying views across the city.
19 Lam Son Square.
Tel: (08) 823 4999;
www.caravellehotel.com

New World ★★★★
Built in 1993, it has luxurious rooms and excellent facilities, located near Pham Ngu Lao.
76 Le Lai. Tel: (08) 822 8888; www.
newworldvietnam.com

Majestic ★★★★
A superbly decorated

hotel from the 1920s with charming staff. Some rooms overlook the river.
1 Dong Khoi.
Tel: (08) 829 5517;
www.majesticsaigon.com

Continental ★★★
This historic hotel was the setting for Graham Greene's novel *The Quiet American*, and it still possesses a grand colonial charm.
132–134 Dong Khoi.
Tel: (08) 829 9203; www.
continentalvietnam.com

Le Le ★★
This mini-hotel is popular with tourists and business people, and good value for money.
171 Pham Ngu Lao.
Tel: (08) 836 8686;
lelehotel@hcm.fpt.vn

Hotel 64 ★
Congenial Madame Cuc has perfected a winning formula, with three hotels in the backpackers' area featuring clean rooms, jovial young staff and free lemon juice, coffee, breakfast and dinner.
64 Bui Vien.
Tel: (08) 836 5073;
madamcuc@hcm.vnn.vn

On business

Vietnam is one of the fastest-growing economies in the world, something that will be understandable once you have visited the country. The liberalisation of the economy and the slow dismantling of Communist habits of red tape and bureaucracy is attracting both foreign investment and trade, especially with the United States. There are many opportunities for foreign companies to benefit from new market opportunities, and Vietnam is getting better equipped to work effectively with Western partners.

Business visas

Visas are required to enter Vietnam by all foreigners except those coming from some ASEAN countries; they last one month. The visa process normally takes one week or more and will require the relevant embassy or visa issuing office to liaise with the Immigration Department of Vietnam. Accordingly, a foreign business person should plan well in advance in order to undertake a business trip to Vietnam.

Government involvement

Vietnam continues to make efforts to improve the efficiency of government. Vietnam's National Assembly is restructuring the state bureaucracy, with eight government offices being merged into three super-ministries. In the fight against corruption, Vietnam's civil servants risk being sacked or demoted if they are caught taking bribes in their dealings with the public.

Economic conditions

Vietnam is slowly emerging from the shadows of China in terms of receiving aid, foreign investment and commercial interest. However, the association with China has allowed Vietnam to methodically plan out its development, largely by observing its neighbour. Amongst Southeast Asian countries, Vietnam is well positioned as a potential force in the coming decade, with a high population/high education combination that most resembles Japan's, but with the advantage that it has its own supply of key natural resources, especially oil and gas. However, there is a strong need for basic infrastructure and for the development of the service sector.

The investment environment

A foreign investor who wishes to invest in Vietnam can choose several types of investment. They can establish a new business with their own capital (known as enterprise with 100 per cent foreign-owned capital) or establish a joint-venture with an existing enterprise in Vietnam. The foreign investor can also carry out business affairs under a co-operation contract with an existing enterprise or a government agency or by doing business in some other ways. The Law on Foreign Investment from July 2000 and its regulations made foreign investment in Vietnam much easier.

Law

Since 1986, Vietnam has been transforming itself from a centrally planned economy into a market economy, facilitated by various Acts and Codes of the State. Vietnamese commercial law provides the legal basics for foreign companies to set up their outlets in Vietnam as company branches, or by appointing Vietnamese agents. However, the legal system is prone to frequent changes and business people are advised to check government regulations carefully.

Communications

Vietnam is putting considerable effort into the modernisation and expansion of its telecommunications system, but its performance continues to lag behind that of its more modern neighbours. All provincial exchanges are digitalised and connected to Hanoi, Da Nang and Ho Chi Minh City by fibre-optic cable or microwave radio relay networks. Since 1991, the number of main lines in use has been substantially increased and the use of mobile telephones is growing rapidly. There is a large number of internet cafés in most towns and luxury hotel chains are equipped with modern business facilities.

Conventions and exhibitions

Trade shows and exhibitions are an important part of making business contacts in Vietnam. Major trade shows are very well attended, which is not surprising in a country deprived of quality products for so long. Contact the Chamber of Commerce (*see opposite*) for more information.

Etiquette

For many foreign business people in Vietnam, business can be frustratingly slow to develop, requiring numerous meetings and approvals from multiple business managers or government ministries. A gentle and respectful attitude is very important and patience will be required in any dealings.

It is recommended to be generous when hosting guests – if faced with a seemingly ungrateful guest (gratitude is sometimes not overtly expressed), don't place too much importance on this. Before meetings, prepare enough small gifts to be presented to each attendee, or, at least, to the main host. It is important to become knowledgeable in the out-of-office business dealings that Asian business people regularly practise, for example entertaining at karaoke bars and talking business over drinks. Many deals are actually sealed with key people in this manner. Incidentally, the black market linked to establishments that cater for business people has been valued at US$2 billion.

Opening hours

Vietnamese tend to rise early and go to bed early. Many shops are open at 7 or 8am and close between 4 and 5pm. Lunch is taken very seriously and most things shut down between noon and 1.30pm, including banks. Government workers take even longer lunch breaks. It is considered bad form to disrupt someone's meal schedule, especially at lunchtime.

Trade

In general, import–export activities are quite open now in Vietnam. Businesses can import or export goods directly, in conformity with their business registration certificate, with only one requirement, which is that they must register for an import–export code at the customs office. The Trade Agreement between the United States and Vietnam, signed recently, also provides easier access to the Vietnamese market for foreign investors.

Further information and useful addresses

There is a host of web resources that give advice on doing business in Vietnam, as well as useful links to other websites. Doing a search for the information you require usually works. The below addresses are a good starting point for the relevant government and business bodies:

Chamber of Commerce and Industry
9 Dao Duy Anh, Hanoi. Tel: (84-4) 5742125. Fax: (84-4) 5742020.
Ministry of Commerce
31 Trang Tien St, Hanoi. Tel: (84-4) 8253094. Fax: (84-4) 8264696.
General Department of Customs
162 Nguyen Van Cu St, Hanoi. Tel: (84-4) 8272551. Fax: (84-4) 8725905.
Central Foreign Trade Bank
49 Ly Thai To St, Hanoi. Tel: (84-4) 8257563.
Branch of Chamber of Commerce and Industry
171 Vo Thi Sau St, Dist. 3, HCM City. Tel: (84-8) 9325904.
Viet Nam Foreign Trade Bank in Ho Chi Minh City
29 Ben Chuong Duong St, Dist. 1, HCM City. Tel: (84-8) 8295652.
Investment and Foreign Trade Development Center
96 Nguyen Hué Blvd, Dist. 1, HCM City. Tel: (84-8) 8231530.

The former French town hall, now the People's Committee Building, HCM City

Practical guide

Arriving

Formalities

All foreign nationals need a visa to enter Vietnam. They can be obtained through Vietnamese embassies abroad. Tourist visas are generally valid for 30 days, cost US$30–100, and take seven to ten days to process. In Southeast Asia, Bangkok is the most popular place to apply for a Vietnamese visa (four to five working days). You'll need to specify whether you need a 'Single Entry' visa, or a 'Multiple Entry' visa that allows you to leave Vietnam and re-enter without having to obtain another visa.

On arrival, you'll need to hand over a completed Arrival and Departure Card. Note that if you're arriving with more than US$3,000, you'll need to declare it on this form. Customs keep the top white copy and you keep the yellow copy: you'll need to hand this yellow form in when you leave the country, and it is also used, along with your passport, for registering at hotels.

Some internal journeys are best made by plane

Visa extensions were being issued through tour agents and travellers' cafés in Ho Chi Minh City, Nha Trang, Hoi An, Hué, Da Nang and Hanoi, but check with the embassy before you leave. The fine for overstaying your visa varies.

By air

Many international airlines fly to Vietnam. Most require a change at one of the major Southeast Asian cities such as Singapore, Kuala Lumpur or Bangkok. The latter has emerged as the principal embarkation point for Vietnam.

Ho Chi Minh City's (Saigon) Tan Son Nhat Airport is Vietnam's busiest international air hub, followed by Hanoi's Noi Bai Airport. A few international flights also serve Danang. Departure tax is US$12, which can be paid in Vietnamese Dong or US dollars.

By land

It is possible to enter Vietnam from Cambodia, China and Laos, and you should not have a problem if you have a valid visa. Make sure you have currency or at least US dollars before you cross, as there are no official exchange facilities and the black market money changers are poor value.

For getting to/from China, it's become very popular to cross the border at Friendship Pass, or Dong Dang, 20km (12$^{1}/_{2}$ miles) north of Lang

Son in northeast Vietnam, to get to and from Nanning. There is a twice-weekly international train between Beijing and Hanoi that stops at Friendship Pass. The other popular border crossing with China is at Lao Cai in northwest Vietnam, which lies on the railway line between Hanoi and Kunming in China's Yunnan Province. There's also a seldom-used crossing at Moi Cai.

It's possible to enter Laos from Lao Bao in north-central Vietnam. There is an international bus from Danang to Savannakhet (Laos). The other crossing is at Keo Nua Pass/Cau Treo, west of Vinh. The only crossing to Cambodia is via Moc Dai. An international bus links Phnom Penh with Ho Chi Minh City.

Camping

There are very few facilities for camping in Vietnam. Many local authorities prohibit foreigners from camping. However, beach resorts seem to be more welcoming of campers, particularly the beachfronts at Mui Ne and Nha Trang.

More popular are home stays with villagers in ethnic minority communities or in the Mekong Delta. In the north or central highlands, staying in a stilt house is an experience, usually consisting of a mattress, blanket and mosquito net, in a communal room. In the Mekong Delta, you can arrange to stay with owners of fruit orchards.

Climate

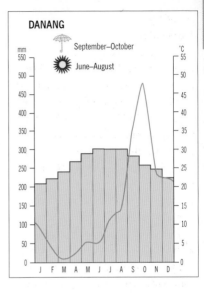

DANANG

September–October

June–August

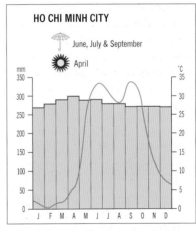

HO CHI MINH CITY

June, July & September

April

Practical guide

WEATHER CONVERSION CHART

25.4mm = 1 inch

°F = 1.8 × °C + 32

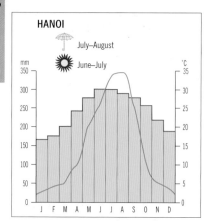

HANOI

July–August

June–July

mm 350 300 250 200 150 100 50 0

°C 35 30 25 20 15 10 5 0

J F M A M J J A S O N D

When one region is wet, cold or steamy hot, there is always somewhere else in Vietnam that is sunny and pleasant. Basically, the south has two seasons: the wet (May to November, wettest from June to August) and the dry (December to April). The hottest and most humid time is from the end of February to May. The central coast is dry from May to October and wet from December to February. The highland areas are significantly cooler than the lowlands, and temperatures can get down to

freezing in winter. The north has two seasons: cool, damp winters (November to April) and hot summers (May to October). There is the possibility of typhoons between July and November, affecting the north and central areas.

Crime and safety

Vietnam is one of the safest countries in which to travel, and most travellers have no problems. Any crimes against tourists are mostly petty, with violent crime being very rare. That said, there are a few things to be wary of. Some tourist destinations, such as Ho Chi Minh City and Nha Trang, have recently acquired a reputation for bag-snatchers, pickpockets and con artists. Watch your bags in the markets in Ho Chi Minh City and on the beach, especially at night in Nha Trang. Whenever possible, leave your valuables behind in a secure place at your hotel.

If you have anything stolen you'll need to go to the police station nearest

A policeman looks after traffic in the Old Quarter, Hanoi

to the scene of the crime and get the police to write up a report for your insurance company; try to recruit an English-speaker to come with you. Be prepared to pay a 'fee'. Corruption among police and other officials can sometimes be a problem. Very occasionally, trumped-up fines are imposed. But with patience, plus a few cigarettes to hand round, you should be able to bargain fines down considerably.

Vietnam is generally a safe country for women to travel around alone. Most Vietnamese will simply be curious as to why you are on your own. That said, it pays to take the normal precautions, especially late at night, when you should avoid taking a cyclo by yourself. It is better to use a taxi instead. Some non-Vietnamese Oriental women travelling with a white man have reported cases of harassment – attributed to the fact that some Vietnamese men assume they are local prostitutes.

Not surprisingly, the Vietnamese authorities are sensitive about military installations, border regions, military camps, bridges, airports and train stations. Anyone taking photographs near such sites risks having the film or memory card removed from their camera, or the ubiquitous 'fine'. Unexploded mines still pose a serious threat, the area most risky being the Demilitarised Zone, where each year a few local farmers are killed or injured. Always stick to well-trodden paths and

CONVERSION TABLE

FROM	TO	MULTIPLY BY
Inches	Centimetres	2.54
Feet	Metres	0.3048
Yards	Metres	0.9144
Miles	Kilometres	1.6090
Acres	Hectares	0.4047
Gallons	Litres	4.5460
Ounces	Grams	28.35
Pounds	Grams	453.6
Pounds	Kilograms	0.4536
Tons	Tonnes	1.0160

To convert back, for example from centimetres to inches, divide by the number in the third column.

MEN'S SUITS

UK	36	38	40	42	44	46	48
Rest of Europe	46	48	50	52	54	56	58
USA	36	38	40	42	44	46	48

DRESS SIZES

UK	8	10	12	14	16	18
France	36	38	40	42	44	46
Italy	38	40	42	44	46	48
Rest of Europe	34	36	38	40	42	44
USA	6	8	10	12	14	16

MEN'S SHIRTS

UK	14	14.5	15	15.5	16	16.5	17
Rest of Europe	36 37		38	39/40	41 42		43
USA	14	14.5	15	15.5	16	16.5	17

MEN'S SHOES

UK	7	7.5	8.5	9.5	10.5	11
Rest of Europe	41 42		43	44	45	46
USA	8	8.5	9.5	10.5	11.5	12

WOMEN'S SHOES

UK	4.5	5	5.5	6	6.5	7
Rest of Europe		38	38 39	39	40	41
USA		6	6.5	7 7.5	8	8.5

never touch any shells or half-buried chunks of metal.

Customs regulations

On arrival in Vietnam, you must complete white-and-yellow duplicate arrival/departure forms. The yellow copy is to be kept with your passport at all times. Hotels and private hosts must register overnight guests with the local police.

Duty-free limits are:
• Cigarettes: 400
• Cigars: 100
• Tobacco: 100g.
• Liquor: 1.5 litres.
• Perfume and jewellery for personal use.
• Small gift items valued at not more than US$ 300.
• Personal effects of a reasonable quantity.
Materials under declaration include:
• Foreign currency in excess of US$3,000
• Gold and jewellery not for personal use.
CDs and tapes are often retained for screening, and will be returned after a few days.

Driving

Driving a car in Vietnam is not yet an option for tourists. However, it is easy to rent a vehicle with driver for the day, from tour agencies. They can tailor-make day trips or longer tours specifically for your needs. It is only really economical if there are more than two of you in a group.

Motorbikes and bicycles can be hired in most towns, and this is quite a popular method of getting around. It is not recommended to hire a motorbike for long distances though, as roads can be quite dangerous. In the big cities, riding a motorbike or bicycle is not for the faint-hearted. Road discipline is virtually nonexistent and the sheer volume of traffic is daunting at times.

If you have an accident, it is customary for both parties to blame each other until someone pays money to the other. As a foreigner, the best way to avoid having to pay is to say that you will call the police to sort it out. Most Vietnamese will not want to be involved with this and will drop the matter.

Electricity

Electricity is 220V, 50Hz. Most plugs are two-pin with rounded pins, although you may come across sockets requiring two flat pins. Power supplies are sometimes erratic, with the occasional electricity cut.

Embassies and consulates
Vietnamese embassies worldwide
Australia
6 Timbarra Crescent, Malley Canberra, ACT 2606. Tel: 26286 6059; Fax: 26286 4534. www.au.vnembassy.org

The Foreign Ministry building

Canada

226 Maclaren Street, Ottawa, Ontario, K2P OL6. Tel: 613 236 0772; Fax: 613 236 2704; E-mail: Vietnam@Istar.ca

UK

12–14 Victoria Road, London W8 5RD. Tel: 0207 937 1912; Fax: 0207 937 6108. www.vietnamembassy.org.uk

USA

1233, 20th Street, N.W. Suite 400 Washington DC, 20036. Tel: 202 861 0737; Fax: 202 861 0917; http://www.vietnamembassy-usa.org

Foreign embassies and consulates in Vietnam

Australia

Embassy: *8 Dao Tan, Hanoi. Tel: 831 8635, 831 8726; Fax: 831 7755.*
Consulate: *5B Ton Duc Thang, District 1, Ho Chi Minh City. Tel: 829 6035; Fax: 829 6031.*

Canada

Embassy: *31 Hung Vuong, Hanoi. Tel: 734 5000; Fax: 734 5049.*

New Zealand

Consulate: *41 Nguyen Thi Minh Khai, District 1, Ho Chi Minh City. Tel: 226906; Fax: 822 6904.*

UK

Embassy: *31 Hai Ba Trung, Hanoi. Tel: 936 0500, 936 0550; Fax: 936 0562.*
Consulate: *25 Le Duan, District 1, Ho Chi Minh City. Tel: 829 8433; Fax: 829 5257.*

USA

Embassy: *7 Lang Ha, Hanoi. Tel: 843 1500/09, 835 0445/49; Fax: 843 1510.*
Consulate: *51 Nguyen Dinh Chieu,*

District 1, Ho Chi Minh City. Tel: 829 2750. Also at 4A Le Duan, District 1, Ho Chi Minh City. Tel: 822 0617; Fax: 822 9434.

Emergency telephone numbers

Try to get a Vietnamese-speaker to phone for you. The main numbers are: Police 113, Fire 114, Ambulance 115.

Health

There are quite a few diseases prevalent in Vietnam that are not yet under the same degree of control as in other countries in Southeast Asia. However, if you take precautions, you are unlikely to suffer major health problems. No vaccinations are currently required for Vietnam although the recommended jabs include typhoid, hepatitis A, tetanus and polio. It is worth remembering to take your malaria pills a week before you travel.

Pharmacies can generally help with minor injuries or ailments, and in major towns you may well find a pharmacist who speaks French or even English. Both Ho Chi Minh City and Hanoi now have reasonably well-stocked pharmacies. That said, drugs past their shelf life and even counterfeit medicines are rife, so inspect packaging carefully, check use-by dates and bring anything you know you're likely to need from home.

Local hospitals will treat minor problems, but in a real emergency your best bet is to get a taxi to Hanoi or Ho Chi Minh City, where excellent

Language

Vietnamese (Kinh) is the official language of the country, although there are dialectic differences across Vietnam. There are dozens of different languages spoken by various ethnic minorities, and Khmer and Laotian are spoken in some parts. The most widely spoken foreign languages in Vietnam are Chinese (Cantonese and Mandarin), English, French and Russian, more or less in that order. English is widely spoken wherever there are tourists, e.g. hotels, restaurants in big towns and tour offices. Many older people speak French rather than English, but most young people learn English at school, so you are rarely going to be unable to communicate, except perhaps in the more remote areas of Vietnam.

BASICS

Vietnamese was originally written using Chinese characters, but a Romanised script was developed in the 17th century, and is used today for everyday Vietnamese text e.g. street signs and newspapers.

It is a tonal language, in which a word's meaning depends on the pitch at which you say the word. Six tones are used, with syllables in writing marked with accents. The scope for misunderstanding is endless. For example, the spoken word Quy can mean 'monster', 'precious' or 'kneeling'. The six tones used are: mid-level tone (syllables with no marker), the low falling tone (syllables marked with à), the low rising tone (syllables marked with ạ), the high broken tone (syllables marked with mã), the high rising tone (syllables marked with má), and the low broken tone (syllables marked with mả).

GETTING AROUND

Where is ...?	Ở đâu ...?
Ticket	Vé
Train	Xe lửa
Bus	Xe buýt
Airport	Sân bay
Train station	Ga xe lửa
Bus station	Bến xe buýt
How do I get to?	Tôi phải đi ... bằng cách nào?
We'd like to go to ...	Chúng tôi muốn đi ...
To the airport please	Làm ơn dưa tôi đi sân bay
Can you take me to the ...?	Ong/bà có thể dưa tôi đi ...?
When does the bus leave for Hoi An?	Khi nào xe Hội An chạy?
How long does it take?	Phải tôn bao lâu?
Aeroplane	Máy bay
Boat	Tàu bè
Train station	Bến xe lửa
Taxi	tắc xi
Car	xe hơi
Bicycle	xe đạp
Baggage	hành lý
Bank	Nhà băng
Post Office	sở bưu diện

Passport	hộ chiếu
Hotel	khách sạn
Restaurant	nhà hàng
Please stop here	xin dừng lại đây
Over there	bên kia
Here	đây
Left/right	bên trái/bên phải
North/South	phía bắc/phía nam
East/West	phía đông/phía tây

EMERGENCIES

Can you help me?	Ông/bà có thể giúp tôi không?
There's been an accident	Có một vụ tai nạn
Please call a doctor	Làm ơn gọi bác sĩ
Hospital	Bệnh viện
Police station	Đồn công an

GREETINGS AND BASIC PHRASES

Hello	Chào ông/bà
How are you?	Ông/bà có khỏe không?
Fine, thanks	Tôi khỏe cám ơn

Yes	Có/vâng/dạ	Laundry	Quân ào dơ
No	Không	Open/closed	Mở cửa/đóng cửa
Thank you	Cám ơn		
Thank you very much	Cám ơn nhiều	**EATING & DRINKING**	
Please	Làm ơn	How much is it?	Bao nhiêu tiền?
Excuse me (to say sorry)	Xin lỗi	Cheers	Can chen (north), Can ly (south)
Excuse me (to get past)	Xin ông/bà thứ lỗi	Ice	Đá
Goodbye	Tạm biệt	No ice, thanks	Không dá cám ơn
Goodnight	Chúc ngủ ngon	Chopsticks	Đũa
I do not understand	Tôi không hiểu	A little sugar	Ít đường
How do you say this in English?	Cái này tiếng Anh nói thế nào ?	Cold	Lạnh
		Hot	Nóng
Do you speak English?	Ông/bà biết nói tiếng Anh không ?	Vegetarian	Người ăn chay
		I don't eat meat	Tôi không được ăn thịt
English	Anh	Delicious	Rất ngon
French	Pháp, táy	Fish	Cá
I	Tôi	Beef	Bò
We	Chúng tôi	Chicken	Gà
You (singular, familiar)	Anh (m), Chị (f)	Pork	Lợn (north), Heo (south)
You (singular, formal)	Ông (m), Bà (f)	Vegetables	Rau co/Rau các loi
You (plural)	Các ông (m), Các bà (f)	Shrimp/prawn	Tôm
They	Họ	Bread	Bánh mì
What is your name?	Tên là gì?	Butter	Bơ
		Cheese	Phó mát ơ
		Chilli	Ót khô
NUMBERS		Egg	Trứng
Zero	không	Beer	Bia
One	một	Coffee	Cà phê
Two	hai	Coffee with milk	Cà phê sữa nóng (south), Cà phê nâu nóng (north)
Three	ba		
Four	bốn		
Five	năm	Black coffee	Cà phê đen nóng
Six	sáu	Tea	Trà (south), Chè (north)
Seven	bay	Water	Nước
Eight	tám	Milk	Sữa
Nine	chín	Orange juice	Nước cam
Ten	mười		
		TIME	
ACCOMMODATION AND SHOPPING		What's the time?	Mấy giờ rồi?
		Today	hôm nay
Hotel	Khách sạn/Hotel	Tomorrow	mai
Room	Phòng	Yesterday	hôm qua
Do you have any rooms?	Ông/bà có phòng không?	Now	bây giờ
How much is it?	Bao nhiêu tiền?	Next week	tuần tới
Can I have a look?	Xem có được không?	Last week	tuần vừa qua
I want a ...	Tôi muốn một ...	Morning	buổi sáng
That's too expensive	Đắt quá	Afternoon	buổi chiều
Bill please	tính tiền	Evening	buổi tới
Do you have anything cheaper?	Ông/bà còn gi rẻ hơn không?	Night	ban đêm
		Hour	giờ
Cheap/expensive	Rẻ/đắt	Minute	phút
Mosquito net	Cái màn	Day	ngày
Toilet paper	Giấy vệ sinh	Week	tuần
Telephone	Diện thoại	Month	tháng
		Year	năm

international medical centres can provide diagnosis and treatment. Hospitals expect immediate cash payment for health services rendered. You will then have to seek reimbursement from your insurance company (hang on to receipts).

The major hospitals for treating foreigners are:

Hanoi: *Vietnam-France Hospital, 1 Phuong Mai. Tel: (04) 574 0740.*
Ho Chi Minh City: *Cho Ray Hospital, 201b Nguyen Chi Thanh Rd, District 5. Tel: (08) 855 8794.*

Insurance

Make sure you have adequate travel insurance before you set off, and always read the small print. All loss must be reported to the police and/or hotel authorities within 24 hours and a written report obtained for insurance purposes. This may be difficult to get hold of, but it's necessary.

Internet

In Vietnam you can connect to the internet easily, using the glut of internet cafés that have sprung up in most towns. In more remote regions and smaller establishments check the rate first, as some can charge higher rates. Many internet cafés have facilities for international internet calls, which can be very good value for money.

Lost property

To report the loss or theft of personal belongings, go to the nearest police station or find a policeman. You may have to wait a long time to make your report. Remember to take a photocopy of the main sections of your passport, in case you lose the original.

Maps and directions

The best maps of Vietnam are the International 1:1,000,000 'Travel Map' of Vietnam and the Nelles 1:1,500,000

A typical sign seen in the country's pagodas

map of Vietnam, Laos and Cambodia. The 1:2,000,000 'Vietnam, Cambodia and Laos World Travel Map' from Bartholomew is good, too. Maps can be bought in bookshops and shops in the main tourist towns.

The Rough Guide Vietnam, Cambodia & Laos map at 1:1,200,000 is perhaps the most up to date.

In addresses, where two numbers are separated by a slash, such as 110/5, you simply make for No 110, where an alley will lead off to a further batch of buildings – you want the fifth one. Where a number is followed by a letter, e.g. 117a, you're looking for a single block encompassing several addresses, of which one will be 117a.

Media

The leading daily English-language newspaper is the *Vietnam News*. The weekly *Vietnam Investment Review* and the monthly *Vietnam Economic Times* are also worth reading for an insight into domestic issues; they include supplements with listings of events and venues for Hanoi and Ho Chi Minh City. A free monthly magazine that is very useful for tourists is *Vietnam Discovery*, published by the Vietnam Department of Tourism, which has listings for the main tourist areas. Some foreign newspapers and magazines are on sale at large bookshops and hotels in Hanoi and Ho Chi Minh City.

The government radio station is the Voice of Vietnam, which became famous during the American War.

Vietnamese currency, 200 Dong note

English-language programmes are broadcast on VOV5 (105.5 MHz). To keep in touch with international news, a short-wave radio is needed for access to world service channels such as the BBC. Many hotels have satellite TV in rooms, showing CNN, MTV and other international channels. VTV1, the main local channel, presents news in English at 2pm and 6pm daily.

Money matters

It is a good idea to bring a small calculator with you for currency conversions, as it can be difficult to calculate things in your head when changing money or assessing the value of something.

Budget

Travellers staying in budget accommodation and eating in small cafés should be able to get by on around US$20 to US$25 per day, plus long-distance transport costs. Those wanting to stay in mid-range hotels, eat out at moderate restaurants, charter occasional taxis and enjoy the nightlife should budget on around US$65 a day.

Hotels vary enormously in price, depending on the type of accommodation, location and town. There is often scope for negotiation, especially out of high season or if you stay more than two nights. Rates are around US$6–15 for a room in a budget hotel, US$15–50 in a mid-range hotel and US$50 upwards for a hotel of four-star standard or above.

Eating out is incredibly good value, and will be one of the pleasures of your trip. Meals will cost US$1–2 for budget places, US$3–8 for mid-range, and US$20 or more for top restaurants.

Credit cards
Visa, MasterCard, American Express and JCB credit cards are accepted in the major cities and towns popular with tourists, although a commission rate is chargeable, often 3 per cent. It is better to take travellers' cheques.

Currency
The domestic currency is the Vietnamese Dong. It is a good idea to carry Dong with you at all times to pay for everything except larger purchases such as hotels, restaurant meals, tours, buses and souvenirs, which can be paid for in US dollars. Virtually all businesses, however, will accept payment in Dong, and many display their prices both in US dollars and Dong. It is recommended to take travellers' cheques with you in US dollars, which can be changed in the major cities.

Exchange
There are four ways to exchange currency: at a bank, at authorised foreign exchange bureaux, at hotel reception desks and on the black market. The best rates are offered by banks, but the exchange bureaux are generally more conveniently located and have longer opening hours. The black-market rate is worse than the legal exchange rate, so if you're offered better rates than a bank it's bound to be some sort of scam.

National holidays
1 January New Year's Day
Late January/mid-February (dates vary each year) Tet, Vietnamese New Year (three days, though increasingly offices tend to close down for a full week)
3 February Founding of the Vietnamese Communist Party
30 April Liberation of Saigon, 1975
1 May International Labour Day
19 May Birthday of Ho Chi Minh
June (eighth day of the fourth moon) Birthday of Buddha
2 September National Day
25 December Christmas Day

Opening hours
Basic hours of business are 7.30–11.30am and 1.30–4.30pm. Most offices close on Sundays, and many also close on Saturdays. State-run banks and government offices as a general rule open Monday to Friday, usually closing at weekends. Travellers' cafés and tour agents tend to open early to late every

Temples and pagodas are usually open all week

Hanoi: *87 Tran Hung Dao.*
Tel: (04) 942 2131
Ho Chi Minh City: *110 Nguyen Du,*
District 1. Tel: (08) 823 2617.

Post offices

Most main post offices are open daily usually from 6.30am to 9.30pm. Rates for all post office services are posted up in the main halls. Mail can take anywhere from four days to two weeks in or out of Vietnam. When sending parcels out of Vietnam, take everything to the post office unwrapped and take your passport. You will have to fill in lots of forms, but try to be as detailed as possible when listing what you are sending, as this cuts down on inspection time. Parcels take a couple of weeks by air and a month or two by sea. The post offices in Hanoi and Ho Chi Minh City are:

Hanoi: *75 Dinh Tien Hoang.*
Tel: (04) 824 5231.
Ho Chi Minh City: *125 Hai Ba Trung,*
District 1. Tel: (08) 824 4244.

Public transport

There is a choice of modes of transport between tourist areas. Taking one or two internal flights substantially cuts down on travelling time, useful for those on a tight schedule. Buses between cities are very cheap and quite comfortable on the whole. Trains are a good idea for longer journeys but are generally more expensive and less reliable than buses.

day. Some museums tend to close on Monday. Temples and pagodas occasionally close for lunch but are otherwise open all week and don't close until late evening.

Police

The police do not tend to have a high profile in towns, mainly because crime is relatively rare. Many Vietnamese stay clear of the police because of their reputation for corruption. For example, in road traffic accidents, locals prefer to resolve the situation themselves rather than getting the police involved. If you have anything stolen, you'll need to go to the police station to obtain a report for your insurance. Try to take along an English-speaker, such as a member of staff from your hotel. The main police stations in the two biggest cities are at:

Air

Vietnam Airlines has a near-monopoly on domestic flights, which are pretty good value. The departure tax on domestic flights is about US$1.50, payable in Vietnamese Dong only.

Buses

Vietnam's tourist buses are a very cheap and convenient way to travel between towns. There are several private bus companies, the most famous of which is Sinh Café Tours. They have tourist offices in most towns and are easy to book. Open Tour tickets allow you to hop on and off buses as you wish, between towns that you select. For example, an open-tour ticket between Hanoi and Ho Chi Minh City will cost US$25–45. However, some find that bus travel starts to grate, because of the sheer number of bum-numbing hours required to go anywhere – most bus journeys between major towns take over four hours.

Trains

While train travel is slower and more expensive than bus travel, it is safer, more relaxed and you're likely to have decent legroom. There are several types of train, including the famous Reuinification Express between Hanoi and Ho Chi Minh City. Think twice before you take a crowded, snail-paced local train. It is wise to book your train seats several days in advance, as they do get booked quickly, especially on the popular routes such as Hanoi to Lao Cai (Sapa region), and Hanoi to Hué.

Sustainable tourism

Thomas Cook is a strong advocate of ethical and fairly traded tourism and believes that the travel experience should be as good for the places visited as it is for the people who visit them. That's why we firmly support The Travel Foundation, a charity that develops solutions to help improve and protect holiday destinations, their environment,

Old steam engine at HCM City (Saigon) railway station

traditions and culture. To find out what you can do to make a positive difference to the places you travel to and the people who live there, please visit *www.thetravelfoundation.org.uk*

Telephones

To call abroad from Vietnam, dial 00 then the country code, then the area code minus the first 0, then the number.
The main country codes are:
Australia *61*
Canada *1*
Ireland *353*
New Zealand *64*
UK *44*
USA *1*

Internet cafés are good places to make international calls, as internet calls are cheaper than standard phone lines. Calling direct from hotel rooms costs at least an extra 10 per cent and there's a minimum charge even if the call goes unanswered. If you need a telephone number, the better hotels should have up-to-date directories. Alternatively, try asking in the post office, or calling the Directory Enquiries number.

Useful numbers include:
International Operator *110*
Directory Enquiries *116*
International Prefix *00*
Time Information *117*
Public phones (all card phones) are only found in the main cities. Phonecards can be purchased at the

post office. Some shops or stalls have phones which you can use for a fee.

To call Vietnam from abroad, dial your international dialling code followed by 84 and the area code minus the first 0, and then the number. The most important regional codes include:
Dalat *63*
Hanoi (city) *04*
Ho Chi Minh City *08*
Hué *54*
Sapa *20*

Time

Vietnam is GMT+7. It is 15 hours ahead of Los Angeles, 12 hours ahead of New York, 7 hours ahead of London, 3 hours behind Sydney and 1 hour behind Perth.

Tipping

Tipping is a relatively new phenomenon in Vietnam, and is more common in the south of the country. Gratuities are not usually necessary in backpacker restaurants, but up-market restaurants will often add on a 5 per cent service charge. Leaving a small tip in other restaurants will be greatly appreciated by the staff. Tips for taxi drivers are purely optional (and most appreciated, however small). It is polite to leave a small donation at the end of a visit to a pagoda.

Toilets

Toilets are usually of a good standard, especially in tourist establishments. It is a good idea to carry toilet paper with you wherever you go, as it is sometimes not supplied in local restaurants. In most places, toilet paper is placed in the rubbish bin rather than in the toilet, due to the poor state of the sewerage system. Squat toilets are sometimes used in more remote areas, with the hole in the ground being the most basic. They are flushed by using a bucket to pour water into the hole.

Tourist information

The best sources of information are the many tour operators, especially in Hanoi and Ho Chi Minh City, who can provide all kinds of assistance, from booking hotels to buying bus or plane tickets. They can also sell you tours or arrange for a private car and driver. There are very few state-owned information bureaux. There is a general information telephone number, government-run and in English; dial 1080 (free).

Travellers with disabilities

On the whole, there are few facilities for travellers with disabilities in Vietnam, which is ironic considering the high number of war-wounded. It is important to phone ahead to warn airlines, hotels and tour companies of your requirements. Some luxury hotels have one or two specially-adapted rooms, but on the whole there are few provisions in hotels for wheelchair guests. Getting around can be difficult, especially in cities like Ho Chi Minh City and Hanoi, where the streets can be an obstacle course, even for able-bodied people. Sources of useful information include:

Global access – catering to travellers with disabilities worldwide, this site has useful tips, links and a bulletin board. *www.globalaccessnews.com*

Emerging Horizons Accessible Travel News – a consumer-oriented magazine about accessible travel, whose primary focus is on travel for people with mobility problems. *www.emerginghorizons.com*

New Horizons – the US Department of Transportation provides useful information on air travel and airports for passengers with disabilities. *www.faa.gov/passengers/passengers_ disabilities*

Two excellent websites for travellers with disabilities can be found at *www.radar.org.uk* and *www.sath.org*. RADAR is based in the UK and Sath in the USA.

A tour boat in Halong Bay

Index

Acknowledgements

Thomas Cook Publishing wishes to thank CPA MEDIA/DAVID HENLEY for the photographs in this book, and to whom the copyright belongs (except the following):

PICTURES COLOUR LIBRARY 113a, 125

WIKIMEDIA COMMONS 131 (Lerdsuwa)

WORLD PICTURES 1

Index: STEPHEN YORK

Proofreading: JAN McCANN for CAMBRIDGE PUBLISHING MANAGEMENT LTD

SEND YOUR THOUGHTS TO
BOOKS@THOMASCOOK.COM

We're committed to providing the very best up-to-date information in our travel guides and constantly strive to make them as useful as they can be. You can help us to improve future editions by letting us have your feedback. If you've made a wonderful discovery on your travels that we don't already feature, if you'd like to inform us about recent changes to anything that we do include, or if you simply want to let us know your thoughts about this guidebook and how we can make it even better – we'd love to hear from you.

Send us ideas, discoveries and recommendations today and then look out for your valuable input in the next edition of this title.

Emails to the above address, or letters to Travellers Project Editor, Thomas Cook Publishing, PO Box 227, Coningsby Road, Peterborough PE3 8SB, UK.

Please don't forget to let us know which title your feedback refers to!